VAL KILMER

I'm Your Huckleberry

SIMON & SCHUSTER PAPERBACKS

New York   London   Toronto   Sydney   New Delhi

Simon & Schuster Paperbacks
An Imprint of Simon & Schuster, Inc.
1230 Avenue of the Americas
New York, NY 10020

First Simon & Schuster trade paperback edition April 2021

SIMON & SCHUSTER and colophon are registered
trademarks of Simon & Schuster, Inc.

For information about special discounts for bulk purchases,
please contact Simon & Schuster Special Sales at 1-866-506-1949
or business@simonandschuster.com.

The Simon & Schuster Speakers Bureau can bring authors to
your live event. For more information or to book an event,
contact the Simon & Schuster Speakers Bureau at 1-866-248-3049
or visit our website at www.simonspeakers.com.

Interior design by Lewelin Polanco

Manufactured in the United States of America

3   5   7   9   10   8   6   4   2

Library of Congress Cataloging-in-Publication Data
Names: Kilmer, Val, 1959- author.
Title: I'm your huckleberry / Val Kilmer.
Other titles: I am your huckleberry
Description: New York : Simon and Schuster, [2020]
Identifiers: LCCN 2019058577 (print) | LCCN 2019058578 (ebook) |
ISBN   9781982144890 (hardcover) | ISBN 9781982144913 (ebook)
Subjects: LCSH: Kilmer, Val, 1959- | Actors--United States--Biography.
Classification: LCC PN2287.K66848 A3 2020 (print) |
LCC PN2287.K66848 (ebook) | DDC 791.4302/8092 [B]--dc23
LC record available at https://lccn.loc.gov/2019058577
LC ebook record available at https://lccn.loc.gov/2019058578

ISBN 978-1-9821-4489-0
ISBN 978-1-9821-4490-6 (pbk)
ISBN 978-1-9821-4491-3 (ebook)

CONTENTS

—— vii ——

CONTENTS

CONTENTS

The Pinball Machine

D ear Reader,

    I have a crush on you.

I know that might sound strange, or forward, but it's the truth.

"You get crushes on *everything*, Val," my ex-wife, Joanne, once told me in her proper English manner. "You have a crush on your organic *garden*."

She was right. And to bring up this crush on you is not to woo you—although that may be a bonus—but to share the sound of this small swell in my heart. Your company brings me hope. To envision such a connection between reader and writer may be a fantasy, but it's one I cannot resist. It energizes me. I have felt this Love coming from the world over lately. I have felt this Love from you. Let's call it unity. "Let's call it eloquence." (That's a line from my one-man show, *Citizen Twain*, that I wrote and have been touring for the last five years.) Thank you.

I've been drawn to this buzz as long as I can remember. The beauty of the universe. I let muses, whether people, animals, or places, infuse my life with wonder and mystery. Though I will warn you, with this

———— 1 ————

ever-sparkly north star, it can be hard at times to distinguish sanctity from temptation. In the words of St. Augustine, "Give me chastity and continence, but not yet." Muses or angels have rescued me countless times, and my own inner puckishness has not only defined my art, it has helped me stay alive. I have had from an early age the gift of healing.

You will see this book takes twists and turns. Welcome to the pinball machine of my mind. Here, authenticity lives with eccentricity. A delicious diet, if a bit unsteady. My poems, my puns, my spiritual side trips, and the names of friends, both famous and infamous, dropped along the way—I can't stop myself. I can't help myself. So come along. It's dangerous, but indulge me. We will travel with lightning speed because I've led a lightning-speed life. Let's begin with one of these muses.

Cher.

Former girlfriend.

Forever friend.

Funniest woman I ever met. A consummate artist who displays the attributes of a child, teenager, and sagacious adult, all at once.

Once Cher works her way inside your head and heart, she never leaves. For her true friends, her steadfast love and loyalty never die. We met a lifetime earlier at a time when she was a luminous icon and I was still standing on the sidelines. We had a wild ride, running around the world, and though we'd eventually veer off in different directions, our spirits stayed united.

So when a few years ago I discovered a lump in my throat that turned out to be cancer, Cher couldn't have been more caring. Like millions of other Americans I had been affected by the financial crisis in 2008. I'd been forced to sell my home in New Mexico and rented an aerie cottage on the Malibu coast. But after my ongoing challenges with breathing, she suggested I stay in her guesthouse.

As dedicated followers of *Architectural Digest* know, she commands a Venetian palazzo in Malibu. Only Cher has the chutzpah to re-create the glory of the Italian Renaissance in Southern California. The most unnerving European monarch would deem her guest quarters quite acceptable. I accepted.

Cher has a knack for finding poetry and truth. She is a blazingly fast thinker and just the best company. We cover everything from politics to poetry. Poetry always calms my soul, consuming it and creating it. One morning, I had been reading Baudelaire's *The Flowers of Evil* and listening to the waves crash. I was in love with the line "The inaccessible blue of spiritual heavens," from the poem "Spiritual Dawn."

I had been awake since dawn. Cher invited me up to the grand patio for lunch. The ocean was imbued with a strange blue. Cher was chatty. I was relaxed. Cher dipped out for afternoon errands. Night fell, and I fell asleep. Suddenly I awoke vomiting blood that covered the bed like a scene out of *The Godfather*. I prayed immediately, then called 911. Then alerted my hostess.

Cher stepped in and stepped up and stilled my spirits. And yet even in my grave condition, I saw her scanning the paramedic, who was Gregory Peck drop-dead handsome. Only in Hollywood, right? Despite the fact that I was covered in blood, I caught her eye and bounced my brows like Groucho Marx. *Hubba hubba.* Cher was bashful to be busted but then couldn't help laughing out loud at the audacity. Here we were, joking about beauty and desire, while I looked like a stunt man from Tarantino's *Reservoir Dogs* and, yes, while my life seemed to be in mortal danger. I thought, *You'll have this guy by the stroke of midnight*. We have telepathy, and she opened her iconic mouth, but words failed her. A rarity. We laughed out loud before they finished with my vitals and shut me up with an oxygen mask.

It was a step along the path of gnarly throat challenges, my tongue swollen with blocked lymph passages, ultimately resulting in two tracheotomies and more than one *Godfather* moment. The cancer miraculously healed much faster than any of the doctors predicted. It has taken time, and taken a toll.

I begin with this memory in part to explain my current condition, as so many have expressed concern and natural curiosity. The thing is, when I speak now, I sound like Marlon Brando after a couple of bottles of tequila. It isn't a frog in my throat. More like a buffalo. It is difficult for others to understand what I am saying. My healing is steady, but so far, slow.

Speaking, once my joy and lifeblood, has become an hourly struggle. The instrument over which I had complete mastery is now out of my control. I know the simple action of trusting and affirming Love is not just a healing balm but a primary healing source. It's not a complicated or esoteric practice. We all know what Love can do. Sometimes one must be defiant about the material picture. I'm living proof.

I'm clear that this mind bending is a necessary part of my enlightenment. The more my puffed-up ego is deflated, the lighter I become. Some days I am weighed down. Some days I pray and listen. Some days I am light as air.

Others, not so much. I am a storyteller who has been deprived of his primary tool. So I've focused on listening and am so grateful for the habits of prayer and the ability to trust in its healing that I've developed since childhood. Stay calm and carry on. I am weighed down with worry and physical pain. Clearly I'm vain, but I'm workin' on it, baby, I'm workin' on it. In fact, I've never met anyone who has worked so hard on their vanity. LOL.

I write for relief. I write for healing. I write to view the past more clearly and place myself firmly in the center of Love. I want to get my story out as quickly as possible, but mostly I write because it feels good to share with the world what the world has shared with me.

I write from my perch immersed in the mysterious Hollywood Hills. My stylish little sanctuary was built in 1923, the year my father was born dirt-poor in the dusty panhandle of Texas. My home is over-stuffed with artifacts, piles of books and tabletops of talismans from my distant past: turquoise from New Mexico, rare arrowheads, a ster-ling silver buckle branded with the logo of my family ranch, and hand axes from secret African anthropological sites. I look out the window and see the hills of Hollywood turn from blue to misty gold. On starlit nights I hear melodious sounds wafting through the air from fancy neighbors' parties. This shelter was birthed in the golden age of film-making. I am a grateful disciple of that original vision. I am also a man on a mission.

The mission is healing, and though I have admitted my vanity, I will do my best to steer this mission from vanity to honesty. Honesty is born of pure Love. Love is the divine healer, but to get to pure Love, I have no choice but to follow the path bravely forged by Dante. I have to go through the inferno.

The distance between heaven and hell is the difference between faith and doubt. I have no doubt, for example, that my recent illness shut down professional opportunities that were really not opportuni-ties at all. The universe's rejection is the universe's protection. I have faith that the shift in my physicality is crucial to the growth in my spir-ituality. When one sense weakens, another grows strong. I have more time to play in the metaphysical forests. That leaves me with the task of writing death-defying stories. This hole in my throat, this fat tongue that impedes my speech, this fury I'm feeling, only fuels my commit-ment to a long-form blues that otherwise might be called an autobi-ography. Like the old singer said, you sing the blues to lose the blues.

The blues are never right unless they're raw. The blues are never right unless they also express joy. For joy at overcoming unforeseen obstacles is reason for celebration. This celebratory blues song will cover the full range of my life. Three acts do not apply. Make it ten acts. Make it twenty. Make it whatever it takes to illuminate a life that leads to understanding. I'm excited to revisit that life, excited to try to make sense out of this rapturous nonsense, and even more excited to do so in my naked now. I quote from the Christian Science hymn "Shepherd, Show Me How to Go" by Mary Baker Eddy, "I will listen for thy voice, lest my footsteps stray / I will follow and rejoice, all the rugged way."

Like all true stories, mine includes extreme chiaroscuro, dazzling light and wrenching darkness. But light leads the way. Light might be my one defining motive and the essence of my character, and my early years were simply flooded with it.

PROGRESS PROVES THE INFINITE

I'm saying what we're praying and how it's neighboring delight
To spend an eternity in this hour holding hands throughout the night
Never needing to check for relevance
(Our proof is what we pay for)
We dance across the cosmos
Reflecting purity and purpose from Pulpit and Press
I salute you brothers and sisters
Whose progress
Proves
The Infinite

—Hollywood, California, 2019

Happy Trails to You,
Roy Rogers and Charles Manson

I was born on the last day of 1959. The final breath of a stultifying decade and then the intoxicating swirl of the sixties. I am the middle son of Eugene Kilmer and Gladys Swanette Ekstadt. My older brother, Mark; my younger brother, Wesley.

I was born a mutt—playful, rambunctious, ready to run in absolutely any direction, except the one I was told. Swedish. Irish. Mongolian. Scottish. German. My father always told us our grandmother was Cherokee. Like my origins, I was hopelessly and happily confused. Eugene was an ambitious man born in the ambitious state of Texas. He sold aerospace parts, fuses, and later real estate. He had a small head but broad shoulders. Gladys was beautiful, quixotic. They navigated together from Moline, Illinois, through the lands of the Navajo and the wilderness of New Mexico to sunbaked Chatsworth, California, the primary landscape of my halcyon years. Chatsworth, the least glamorous corner of Los Angeles, sits at the northern border of the San Fernando Valley at the foot of an imposing mountain range. The smoggy suburban sprawl contains a number of anonymous industrial parks where my father found a cheap, giant warehouse to store the materials of his various endeavors, under the umbrella of Liberty Engineering, after *The Statue of*. These were the days before Chatsworth, Canoga Park, and Winnetka became the porn industry mecca of the world.

When I was born, we lived on the beach in Playa del Rey until our whole block was mowed down by the city to make a runway at LAX. Today whenever you fly off into the wild blue yonder, you can see the checkerboard of asphalt that was once my home.

I have memories from before I could speak. I remember brushing my fingers along the bars of my crib. I was plotting my first escape. Once, during an earthquake, a California norm, I crawled beneath our Formica-top kitchen table and felt the rumbling of the earth beneath me. Earthquakes have always excited me, and I remember peeking over the table wondering if the fog would be wiped clean by a giant tidal wave. Seismic shaking, my first encounter with primitive rock

At home in Playa del Rey with older brother, Mark (*foreground*)

and roll. I liked that motion, liked looking through the window with its unobstructed ocean view, liked the mysterious arrival of that heavy fog that made the outside world disappear.

My father was always on his way out the door. Where was he going? And to do what? When I was old enough to ask our eternally smiley nanny, Lulabell, she and my mother both responded in unison, "He's an engineer." "What train?" Oh, how they laughed. I still wonder what train he was on. It was this puzzle of predictably mysterious movement. And then the painful aura of November 22, 1963, when I was three, watching Dad and Mom face the little black-and-white box as Jackie Kennedy stood by, dressed in a suit stained by blood. Something darkened in me because I saw that Dad was shattered. I didn't want a shattered father. I wanted him whole, present, affectionate, loving. I still want that. I still want something that sometimes feels like I can never have, except in spirit.

To many, it would seem as though I grew up wealthy. My father was an operator whose businesses blossomed in ways no one understood but him. He was always ahead of his time, sometimes to a fault. Except for with fashion. Whew. When Dad's blossoms ultimately wilted, I was a young adult. One reason we were always thought to have more means than we did was my father's unfailing generosity. I don't believe I ever sat at a table my father didn't pay for. He fully, even lavishly, financed the first man of color in his business, in direct competition with him, as he worked harder than any man he had met and felt strongly he should be supported at a time when there were virtually no black men in the entire region he lived and worked.

As a kid, I was blessed by an overabundance of energy (unless you were a teacher of mine; then you needed the patience of Job). My mother used to make us bologna sandwiches, kiss us on the head, and wave as we took off on our one-speed Schwinns, often not to come back until after dark. Our legs were so blown out with fatigue by the time we returned, we'd have to walk our bikes up the dirt road, just parallel to Roy Rogers and Dale Evans, one thousand yards from our home. They owned all the property around us, and what they didn't own belonged to one of their closest friends, a man who lost everything and hanged himself in one of the barns. Imagine. What a place to grow up!

We moved from Playa del Rey to Chatsworth, trekking from sand and sea to the golden hot tumbleweeds and oak trees, where the leaves prick you like tarantulas and rattlesnakes and wild peacocks lull you to sleep, along with the fragrance of eucalyptus.

The peacocks are still there. At first they were the treasures of a local rancher who had a weekend rodeo with famed farrier Wilford Brimley. He loved that I knew that about him and he was damn hard to impress. Also that I knew some of the Turtles' original rodeo circuit cowboys. Look 'em up. We made it just under the wire, like I did with the death of film. I was aware of the death of the cowboy right before my baby eyes.

In the Valley, I was a wild thing. I climbed sandstone boulders at great velocity with zero fear. My skin grew back rougher and more resilient each month. I'd scrape it bare with my older brother, who was even stronger than me. He was unreal. When we would catch pickup games in the black community in Palm Springs, it made me so proud that my brother would be chosen in the first couple rounds, as he could slam-dunk almost every time. He was six foot two. Barely. What a pair of springs he had. Such a natural talent, I used to beg him when we were in college to take up dancing. He had that crazy knack for being able to copy movement almost instantly. I could do it with character movement but never in sports. Instead I'd catch toads and create homes for them by bashing holes in the tops of apricot cans. I was ever exploring, ever running. Then we got into engines, riding dune buggies and motorcycles for hours in the baking sun. And my father put us on his lap and let us drive the Cadillac, whose hood seemed like it was halfway home, it was so long.

From our home in Chatsworth, it took at least ninety minutes to get anywhere or do anything. My father was a dreamer full of dichotomies, both arrogant and humble. He was raised in the New Mexico wilderness on trout they caught from the river that ran through their campsite, plus whatever my grandfather shot for food. Beyond that it was cornmeal, grits, beef jerky, Spam, and pinto beans. Once my mother was so frustrated trying to change his prison-lifer palette that she fed him just that for three days straight, pinto beans and Spam. She says he never said a word.

My father was mysterious, too. An only child, LA-citywide math and spelling champ with a singular mix of weakness and strength. As an adult he was starved for excitement; my mother yearned to please him but was often exhausted by the time he got home. He had grown up in the wilderness, where energy meant survival. But my mother was distracted and often detached, from all of us. Her husband was alarmed by the fact that she never bothered to track her children. We could have been anywhere. Once my little brother was lost so long we called the cops. I found him sleeping peacefully under the seat we had had dinner in, in the kitchen. He had enormous energy as well, but had simply hit the wall.

I think it may have been as simple as she knew my father was cheating on her and couldn't handle it and had only her Christian Science practitioner to confide in and to guide her. My folks were never partners. And one of my father's great disparities was his dual and simultaneous stinginess and generosity. He would buy a Cadillac we couldn't yet afford but not let my mom buy curtains for the living

Mom in the 1950s

room. Our home was only ever half furnished because of this Ebenezer Scrooge side of him. So weird.

I remember when rock and roll hit us and hit us hard. Dad, not being a lover of any music he hadn't learned around a campfire and so limited to about eight songs, wouldn't let us buy more than one record a week between the three of us at the height of rock's steamrolling, earth-soaking prowess. How could we decide between the latest Beatles record and the latest hard-rock experimental Jimi Hendrix experience, or the latest Sly and the Family Stone masterpiece, or Stevie Wonder? Oh, what perfect hell. And this, again, was when my father was making stacks.

The lack of such structure made it tempting to run away. I once did, when we were still living at the beach. I was three when I asked Mom to show me how to capture butterflies and moths and make the holes in the tin tops to the glass jars we stored fruit in from our couple of trees. But Mom, giggling with a girlfriend on the phone, paid me no mind. I was crushed and decided to leave once and for all. Mom didn't even notice when I grabbed my GI Joe backpack and tiny plastic tent and indignantly announced that I was never returning home. If she wanted to see my new digs, I'd be living under the tree in the empty lot next door. Still on the phone, she only half-heard my gallant farewell speech. I was burning with anger.

The adventure was arduous, about thirty feet away, and the day scalding hot. The lot was covered in sand. Twenty yards . . . I was uncomfortable and bored. For a few minutes, I rested, watching a caravan of crawling caterpillars. Then, with the smell of Mom's insanely delicious melty chocolate chip cookies wafting through the air, I nearly caved, before I swore to stand my ground, and made it another ten yards to the middle of the sandy lot. For ten minutes. Then twenty. Then thirty. Then . . . enough. The ol' "make me come home 'cause of chocolate cookie smell" was one thing, but the thought of Mom's bologna sandwiches with mayonnaise oozing through the crevices of squishy Wonder Bread . . .

I ran home and felt like I had just docked from New Zealand. But I feigned indifference. She hadn't even noticed I'd gone. The silly story marks a theme that's followed me through life, this dialectic of wandering and grounding, of sacrifice and indulgence, of wonder and bread.

I've run in and out of insanely intense romantic relationships. I've been known to walk through the snow for miles to see a girl or fly across the world at a moment's notice to sit under the African sun with a woman who I knew would—and did—change my molecular makeup. Perhaps like any kid who grew up in the San Fernando Valley, I saw the world happening somewhere else. Not somewhere over the rainbow, no, just somewhere over the Santa Monica Mountains, somewhere over Mulholland Drive. There was a mighty snobbery to the Hollywood geography.

There were only three types of territory. You had to live in Beverly Hills or the Hollywood Hills, or if you were super wild and renegade but still had to have the recognition of stardom or success, you made the trek in from Malibu. Or maybe the real jewels were those tentacles like the Palisades or Holmby Hills, little pockets of opulence. Opulence is a thirty-foot fence made of ancient trees, planted tight as a wicker imprisonment, keeping the paparazzi out, away from the superstar sunbathing in the back as if she were in the south of France or the hills of Tuscany, the rocky slopes of Greece or the Spanish rancheros of the Southwest, all jammed together in a madhouse of hard-earned purchased taste, French nouveau riche next to a super-modern Case Study House. Then there was always the "old money" of Pasadena, which in California terms meant about thirty-eight years old. Then there was the bastion of smarty-pants like Marlon and Warren and Jack and Coppola, who just didn't bother deciding who to please and lived on top of everyone on Mulholland Drive. The older smart real estate mogul actors lived near what was really their own private airport at Burbank, and were like the genius businessman Bob Hope, who owned thousands of acres all over greater Los Angeles. I could feel all this secret wealth swarming around, dusted up into the twister from *The Wizard of Oz*. The studios and the largest backlots were in the Valley as well. I passed Warner Ranch every morning on my way to school. Berkeley Hall on Swall Drive. Boy, I knew it was somewhere else. Even though cowboy superstar Roy Rogers was right next door, he hardly represented what my little heart intuitively understood was deep, soulful acting. Talent, class. My father's idea of success seemed to be a numbers game. He didn't give a whit what his home or its contents looked like, or pleasing our mother with the normal gifts a hardworking housewife who was being cheated on received, like diamonds and pearls and new cars and clothes. And what do you do with those things in the complete isolation of Chatsworth? We were in the witness protection program of culture. Although this great show of absence in parenting from our folks also can rightly be seen as glorious trust that we were okay out on a grand trip of discovery, every day of our eternal summer vacation and after school and the weekends. They created in us all or allowed us all to flourish as ourselves, without a single syllable of judgment. I am eternally grateful for this outstanding gift of self-reliance. I see it now in my own children and am very proud they know the difference as well. Being smothered creatively is some kind of terrible crime our youth suffer from today, being locked into the "rules" of apps and games and the weird madness of control that's clearly out of control these days about our true natures, which are 100 percent evaluated in terms of being a consumer. Well that's no fun at all. Not really. It's somewhere else.

I had to get to that somewhere else. I've always had a starving, stealthy spirit. I want to get up and out. Even back then I wanted to scream my declaration of freedom, though I was painfully shy.

Mom's three sons were born within a period of four years, and I was the apple of her eye. I was told that when Mom gave birth to us, without painkillers or other drugs—you know, the way babies have been born since the dawn of time—she did so without a sound.

Mother was very beautiful, likened often to that greatest of natural talents in film Ingrid Bergman, also Swedish. She was at once a strong woman with strong weaknesses. She had her dark side and seemed to be burdened by aspects of life she was rarely able to convey to my big brother, Mark, and me. She and my father shared an understanding of Christian Science, whose underlying premise has an illuminating simplicity: Always turn from the material to the spiritual. From hate to Love. When *Love* is spelled with a capital L, as I will do often here, it means the Father/Mother Love, the God of All in all. Free of the burden of doctrine that held hell and damnation over the heads of its constituents, Christian Science, founded in 1879 by Mary Baker Eddy, provided comfort to my parents. I inherited their

Christian Science founder
Mary Baker Eddy

faith through hard-fought experimentation and proof.

I've held fast to that faith throughout life, even though my parents never really taught us the practice of it. I recognize, respect, and revere all systems of sacred belief that embrace a golden rule of non-judgment. Christian Science is simply a modern application of ancient Christianity found in the New Testament. It professes the ethos of unrelenting Love and reasserts the lost element of healing largely left out of almost all Christian faiths today, for some reason. Over time, its power transformed from the unconscious to the conscious in my mind. Seems kind of important and useful to me, being able to heal yourself. As a kid, I felt it brewing. As an adult, it has come to full flower. It's a subtle religion by nature, as its main tenets are prayer, study, and solitary, interior acts of tenderness. That doesn't mean I haven't led a frenzied life. That frenzy is still alive and well. It does mean, though, that I have never lost my faith to what seems to me is a kind of materialism that leads nowhere, nowhere of value anyway. Never met a super wealthy person where money obviated any of the basic challenges of finding happiness in the material world. "Money can't buy me love."

My mother's aloofness made me want to please her even more, and she was unique in that she never exploited unconditional Love, as mothers sometimes do. Her Love was an invisible golden thread, something I couldn't always sense, but we were close in the psychic realm. Sometimes she suffered from migraines that I was aware of even across the country when I had moved to New York to study acting and she to a new life with a new husband, Bill, the love of her life, in Wickenburg, Arizona. Other times I could see her riding her horse on the wind and it looked like she was flying. Whenever I called her with these sort of visions, they were inevitably true. She was arty but also conservative, and she grew more so with time.

For both Mom and Dad, life in the Valley was monotonous. A couple times a year, they beat back the boredom by laboring over elaborate themed parties at the house. One night, our home was transformed into Monte Carlo's most sophisticated casino. I snuck out of my tiny bed. I may have even stuffed the bed with pillows, gettin' the idea from some movie. I spent the night sandwiched in between an itchy wall that scratched right through my flannel PJs and our floral sofa, looking up at the wild transformation of our normally unadorned living room. It was full-on midsixties orange Day-Glo, with cardboard cutouts everywhere. Pin the tail on the go-go dancer. Young moms were letting their hair down, housewives rocking out in their miniskirts, and aerospace engineers letting their long lapels hang low. Everywhere I looked the topography was red, yellow, and leather. I swooned at the dancing, bedazzled by the makeshift costumes, until I was captured and scolded.

We lived next door to Roy Rogers and too close for comfort to Charles Manson. We used to go to Spahn Ranch, where they all lived. It was the closest place to rent a horse for a trail ride. The guy who put me on his horse was Donald "Shorty" Shea, who worked at Spahn Ranch. He was killed by members of the Manson family a few weeks after the Tate-LaBianca murders, though his body wasn't discovered until 1977. I never saw Manson himself but clearly remember the panic that ran rampant when the grisly murders made international news. It happened when I was eight, but by then the Love vibe, projected by Mom and Dad in different ways, protected us from fear. Whatever deficiencies my parents possessed, they adored their boys.

Roy Rogers was a happier story, mostly. When his ranch went up for sale, Dad bought it and moved us in. When the world's most famous cowboy was still living there, I'd sneak over and peek through the windows of their great room. Inside were Bullet, the German shepherd, and Trigger, Roy's beloved trick horse and invaluable costar, perched on two hind legs. Both animals were quite dead but professionally taxidermied. We couldn't help but worry whether, when his wife, Dale Evans, died, he might stuff her and place her in the kitchen holding a plate of chocolate chip cookies. Fortunately, Dale outlived Roy. Terrible joke, but I was eight. Imagine going to sleep knowing that one neighbor had hanged himself and the other had stuffed two of his three costars.

These hills were home to hundreds of Westerns. Landscapses of imaginary freedom where make-believe cowboys fought fake battles and won real fame and glory. Our local wandering hobo, begging with a paper coffee cup, sang old country tunes. They say your hometown shapes you, and that was mine. The shape had a heroic bent. The lore of heroism, even though it was heroism fashioned by Hollywood, was hidden in the hills above our ranch, etched into the sandstone boulders of Chatsworth, and written on the Santa Ana winds, as Joan Didion describes in her brilliant essay collection on her early times in LA, *Slouching Towards Bethlehem*–the title coming from that powerful poem by W. B. Yeats.

We lived a much more holistic lifestyle than we realized. Orange groves, avocado trees, and hand-churned butter from down the street.

We boys were sent to Berkeley Hall, a Christian Science school.

Roy Rogers with a stuffed Trigger, 1974

And though my father's relationship to spirit was not salient, I drank in the mystery of faith. As early as I can remember, I curated this notion of an all-loving force, a messiah both male and female. In coming years, I would eventually tear through the Bible, the Bhagavad Gita, and the Qur'an, searching for either a new faith or proof that what I was born into was a true solid foundation to build a life on. But I kept coming back to the love of Love, the most reliable rule that I ever knew. I also kept coming back to Mrs. Eddy, who was so egalitarian in her Love that she spent a year writing God with exclusively feminine pronouns. The next year she reverted; her publisher must have realized the world wasn't ready for a female God. She reasoned that we have much more cause to consider God feminine than masculine, as the leading qualities of Love, empathy, compassion can be more easily found in a woman than a man or a feminine makeup than masculine. I've always found women infinitely more interesting than men. Perhaps that's why we've always gotten along so well. I have never suffered the illusion there was any winning with a woman. We are big oafy elephants in the room and they are butterflies. And it takes so long for an elephant to get to asking a question of relevance to a butterfly. Thanks for being so patient, ladies. We're trying to catch up, we really are . . .

Grandpa Kilmer's Grave
in Truth or Consequences

I was a feral wanderer, yearning for lightness. I searched for something strange yet wholly comforting. Reading came quickly. The first poem of my heart was written by a distant cousin who had died in 1918. It turned out to be a famous verse because of its profound simplicity. I read Joyce Kilmer's "Trees" out loud to my second-grade class.

> I think that I shall never see
> A poem lovely as a tree.
>
> A tree whose hungry mouth is prest
> Against the earth's sweet flowing breast;
>
> A tree that looks at God all day,
> And lifts her leafy arms to pray;
>
> A tree that may in Summer wear
> A nest of robins in her hair;

Upon whose bosom snow has lain;
Who intimately lives with rain.

Poems are made by fools like me,
But only God can make a tree.

Kilmer was a devout Catholic and his spiritual nature is reflected in the piece. He was a war hero who sacrificed his life defending democracy during World War I in France, which made his poem all the more easier to be chosen as the first piece representing the genre of writing when our textbooks became nationalized across the USA.

As much as I've strived to infuse meaning into the poems and plays I've written throughout my life, the fully blossomed tree is the ultimate book, poem, and play. When in *A Midsummer Night's Dream* Puck tells his king, "Lord, what fools these mortals be!" I believe Shakespeare had himself in mind. The Bard knew that art is essentially artifice–lovely artifice, enchanting artifice, but artifice nonetheless. There's absolutely nothing artificial about a tree.

When Shakespeare offers his most salient beliefs about how to find value in this life, he suggests through Hamlet that it is the actor's charge "to hold the mirror up to nature . . . to show the very age and body of its time, its form and pressure." The actor's job, in other words, is to show us who we really are, and as a smarter man than me has noted, if we don't learn from history we are destined to repeat it. The experience of acting Shakespeare makes clear, throughout his impossibly diverse attempts to clarify and elucidate our souls to us, that we've got the best, most condensed shot at understanding the truth of our very spirit through a display or reflection of actions that reveal our habits and folly as well as our nobility and higher strivings. Although he's a haughty one, that ol' Bill, he's a naughty one.

I came to learn that Mark Twain had wisdom not unlike Shakespeare's. He understood that, like everyone, he fell into foolery. He also saw how artificial language could be. So he changed up the language and made it real. More than a couple of scholars say that's the start of gutbucket American lit. I didn't know all that when, as a kid, I first met Huckleberry Finn. All I knew was that I loved his story. First time I read it, I was in what felt like an enchanted forest of pine trees. Leaves fell gracefully on my shoulders; mosquitoes nibbled at my ankles. I was Huck. Jim was my playmate. Together we floated on the raft, the Mississippi holding us aloft. Fleeing the civilized world, scorned by polite society, speaking an intoxicating patois that had my head reeling, I joined Huck and Jim on every one of their crazy adventures. Twain struck a visceral chord, perhaps a lifetime's worth of chords. He railed against divisions of race, class, and age. He was coarse and brilliant and funny and irreverent and honest and, as someone who deserted the Confederate army two weeks after joining, a famous coward. I came to love all these contradictions.

Grandma, a true American, was a character out of Twain. She was down-home and funky. Dad instilled within me a small fear of his mother's empty coffee can that stood next to her feet. "Never look inside that can," he warned. And of course, I couldn't resist. Curiosity over fear.

I must have been three when I approached that forbidden can. Grandma couldn't stop sucking on her corncob pipe. Beyond smoking like a chimney, she was hooked on snuff. She pinched finely ground tobacco and snorted it right up the schnoz. She also chewed tobacco. Her spittoon was the forbidden coffee can at the foot of her rocker. When I took the plunge and breathed in that dank, brackish, murky muddle of old tobacco chew and sinewy saliva, my stomach churned.

Churning, yearning to bring back memories like Grandma's scar.

They say every scar tells a story. I'd stare at the scar that sat on her right shoulder–it's one of my first memories–and wonder how it came about. Dad told the tale. His father, whom I never knew, was a prospector. He lived till one hundred. Amazingly, he was sixty when Dad was born. I never asked, but I presume Grandma had to be many more than ten years younger than her husband. A gold prospector, Grandpa Thomas explored, drilled, and excavated mineral deposits.

He died in Hot Springs, New Mexico–later renamed Truth or Consequences after Ralph Edwards, host of a radio game show by that name, promised to broadcast an episode from any town that changed its name to that of the show.

The legend of my grandparents' past loomed large in my imagination. The camp where they prospected was attacked by Native Americans. An arrow was shot into Grandma's shoulder, a tomahawk smashed into Grandpa's skull. Grandma, with the help of a local

Grandpa Kilmer outside his cabin in New Mexico

Mexican, managed to get him in the back of their wagon, hitch the horse and mule, and ride through the wilderness until she found a doctor, who put a metal plate in her husband's head. Winters used to drive him crazy as the plate was always cold.

When I was still a preteen, Dad took me to what had been the cabin my grandfather built on Zuni land, now a national park in New Mexico, where I stared at a hummingbird. Soon the bird was joined by another. And then another. And then another, until there were at least a hundred hummingbirds flying overhead. I felt as though I had conjured them. I knew that one day, like Grandpa, I would live in the New Mexican wilderness.

Grandpa was also a mountain man. Think *The Treasure of the Sierra Madre*. He lived on beans and berries. Grandma eventually gave up on him and moved to Los Angeles, but Grandpa was always coming to LA and stealing my dad back to the mountains to help him with his prospecting. Eventually my concerned grandmother would hide Dad rather than have her ex-husband drag him back into the wilderness. The danger of freezing to death was real. My father eventually confronted Grandpa. He liked school and was good at it. From what I gathered, this was such an alien idea to my grandfather. He could find no good reason to have that kind of mind around him in the wilderness. Besides, he was getting old. And feeding a young giant was expensive. My father was six foot three by his third year in high school.

When in the sixties I visited Pueblo Park Campground at the northern edge of the Blue Range Wilderness, the cabin my grandfather built was still standing, with arrowheads, pottery shards, and stray bits of turquoise strewn about in the leaves and grass. Dad never tired of telling the story about facing a bear in the woods. It was only a cub, but then again, so was my dad. He screamed and ran like the wind. He couldn't get the little bear off his mind. Grandpa had gone off on a trip, and Dad felt an obligation to protect his mother. He imagined the cub growing up to become a killer grizzly. He took it as his duty to get that bear before the bear came back to get him. Screwing up his courage, he grabbed his dad's rifle from the closet when Grandma wasn't looking and went searching for the creature. He had been gone for hours when Grandma grew alarmed. She could easily track him because a single line in the dirt marked the path along which he'd dragged the rifle, too heavy for his small frame. When his mother found him, he had fallen asleep under a ponderosa pine, cuddling the rifle like a teddy. I love imagining my father, so ferocious in his later life, as a sweet little boy lost in the woods, dreaming heroic dreams of slaying beasts and becoming a man.

More Kilmer lore: Grandpa Thomas delivering his mule to a man whose horse had died, risking his own work and life by giving away this animal but adhering to the sacred code that in the wilds everyone is connected and responsible for one another. You do whatever your neighbor needs at whatever cost to you—a bit more than just bringing over a pie when you move in, which isn't even practiced anymore in society. It's a beautiful way of living. I have both offered and received this remarkable kindness from people for all the decades I have lived in the New Mexico wilderness. You are valued by what you do, not who you are or how many cars or backhoes you own.

When they were quite young, I took my daughter, Mercedes, and son, Jack, on a trip to search for Grandpa Thomas's grave. The return to Truth or Consequences turned mystical. I went to the records office to study the cemetery map soiled with the exotic dirt that had buried our ancestors. It was too dark to go to the cemetery. That would wait till tomorrow. That night the kids and I slept in a rented Winnebago. Mercedes woke with an earache as numbing as a gunshot wound, the pain unbearable, subsiding only enough to let her moan and sweat. A day earlier, we'd gone below sea level into the colorful Carlsbad Caverns, as dramatic an adventure as nature could design, and now we were miles from Western medicine. I did all I could to comfort her.

Meanwhile, I was up most of the night, scrutinizing a copy of the old cemetery map, imagining my grandfather's flight across Tennessee and Texas to New Mexico as he dreamed of gold. Grandpa found it—or did he? Did he die defending it? No, my dad said. He took his riches to Denver, where the bank burned down, destroying his legitimacy. Another story said he was robbed by his own partners. Sometimes I see that thin line—between truth and pure invention—running through the entirety of my family history.

Morning broke. Fortunately, my daughter awoke with a calm ear and mighty appetite. After pancakes, victory! Back at the records office I found Thomas Kilmer's death certificate and that same day discovered his grave. My first thought was to exhume my grandfather's bones and transport them to my ranch in Pecos. I was ready to do it, until I was told by a lawyer that in New Mexico anyone is allowed to visit their dead relatives' remains, regardless of where the land is or who owns it. I didn't love the idea of estranged relatives passing through whenever they damn well pleased. Plan foiled. So instead of shepherding a strange but wondrous excavation, I bought flowers. As I snapped photographs of my kids at Grandpa's grave, I remembered that Dad, although he'd never taken the trouble to find this cemetery, had sworn he'd buy a proper marble tombstone but never did.

The experience was a gentle piercing of the heart. I was unraveling from the carelessness of my ancestors and yet honored and healed by my children, quietly generous and tolerant of this adventure to find a dead man none of us had ever known. We wished him peace.

In the aftermath, a question remains: Why didn't I order a tombstone for Gramps? Why didn't I provide that marble Dad had promised? I honestly don't know. He deserves one. I may have been reluctant because I wasn't clear on what should be written. I wanted to put more than his name, but I also lacked hard information about him.

It was almost easier not knowing my grandfather than knowing my father, who, on some deep level, I also didn't know. I wanted to know more than was allowed me. I wanted to understand how his character so deeply informed my own. When he was nine, my father had picked cotton for a dollar a day. He had watched the man next to him drop dead from exhaustion. That served only to make him pick faster. He was a man who never stopped moving. He drove at a hundred miles per hour as though it were fifty. And, whether he was in a boom or a bust phase of his volatile career, Daddy always had a Caddy. During one boom he ripped up the Valley in a lime-green El Dorado. We'd race from Chatsworth to Palm Springs in seconds.

Dad relished breaking rules. He maniacally maneuvered through the world. I perceived that as normal. I inherited his sense of impetuous movement. His spontaneity was exciting. And without spontaneity I would not have lived the life that I cherish. Dad wanted to be big, bigger, biggest. His great dream was to buy and develop hundreds of acres of land north of the 118 freeway. He saw himself a modern-day William Mulholland, a man destined to leave his mark on Southern California.

Magical thinking, magical realism. Magic bound our family together. That's why we were wild for Disneyland. Three boys, an aspirational dad, an artistic mom, a lonely suburban landscape from which we'd escape down the freeway for fantasy weekends in the less lonely suburb of Anaheim. We went so often it felt like we lived in Disneyland. The only thing that stopped us from staying there for weeks at a time was the monorail. I suppose it makes sense that my father, a man whose vast futuristic vision entailed the ownership of endless acres of land, was claustrophobic. He couldn't sit inside the smooth-moving monorail, the only route from the hotel to the park.

It wasn't the costumed characters that charmed my budding imagination. It was Merlin's Magic Shop shop next to the Sleeping Beauty Castle. That's where I spent hours playing with unbought toys. They were my first props. In top hat and tails, the wily magician performing in front of the shop enacted the first theatrical role I relished. With sleight of hand, he embodied the beauty of magic and commanded his stage. I marveled at the suitcases and boxes from which he pulled scarlet scarves and snow-white bunnies.

I liked mysterious objects—arrowheads my father brought back from New Mexico, pieces of pottery Mom collected. I studied Uncle Dewey's ornate cigarette case and stole a half dozen of his Pall Malls. Each seemed a foot long. I found a box of my own, into which I placed each filterless cigarette at an angle. Come sundown, I scurried up to my treehouse and, for the first time, lit up. The smoke bombed my tiny body. I was probably eight, absolutely oblivious to the catastrophic effects.

I wish I knew even a little of my mother's history. She knew none of it or cared for none of it. She was in this sense remarkably attentive to some of the more difficult instructions of Mrs. Eddy's, like not developing any habits about human history, hence her complete lack of focus on it. Perhaps we have unbelievably fascinating Viking history we just haven't ever explored as a family, or Mongolian, which every Swede has a touch of because when the Huns blasted through and killed all the men, they raped all the women, so there's a line across all of Scandinavia which marks their blood. It's no doubt why I have those weird undeveloped molars inside the lower jaw, and why my older brother, Mark, tans until he is as dark as a blackout. We were not encouraged to contemplate or celebrate birthdays, so I got confused every now and again when hers was.

Older brother Mark had a photographic memory for movement. Had he followed my advice and become a dancer, he'd be legendary. In my mind, he still is. He and I competed at every sport possible: football, baseball, bikes, skateboarding, surfing, go-karts, motorbikes, ice-skating, water-skiing, tennis, rock climbing.

Baby brother Wesley was a genuine genius who, at a startlingly young age, wrote, directed, and produced brilliant homemade films. Oh, Wesley! Mark and I loved Tonka toys. Wesley loved art supplies. He had to create. I had to roll. I was a ball of kinetic energy. I was also impish and a bit mean. If I were to attack my brothers, my weapon was a set of pins from Mom's sewing kit. After I struck, Mark chased me furiously as I hopped over thorny huckleberry patches in our backyard. (I can't help but note how soon in this story huckleberries crop up.) On other occasions, I might shoot Mark with bullets of cork from an air rifle. Sometimes I'd replace the cork with sesame seeds that would fire at lightning speed. Mark was a formidable adversary. Fast as I was, Mark was faster, so fast he'd always catch me and pound me into submission. Our Cain-and-Abel show got off to a fast start.

The soundtrack to all this speed was sixties music. It hit early and it hit hard. I was obsessed with music. Music from the pre-hippie, hippie, and post-hippie epochs, Stones and Doors, Hendrix and Janis, Cream and Bowie, Dylan and Van Morrison, Sly and the Family Stone, soul queen Aretha and soul king James Brown. And of course the Beatles. Music penetrated my soul, drove my engine even faster. I sang morning, noon, and night. Sang myself awake, sang myself to sleep. My heart never stopped singing.

With brothers Mark (*left*) and Wesley (*right*)

From as far back as I can remember, I made up songs. I was thrilled by how *love* rhymed with *dove* and semi-rhymed with *hug*. These early pains and pleasures of creativity were critical to my being. Pains because I couldn't write music but nonetheless heard lilting melodies and lush harmonies. Pleasures because the words spilled from my heart. The words always involved love and longing.

We owned a used upright. I took lessons but never practiced. By the time we got off that school bus from Beverly Hills it was almost night. I was just too tired to practice. In fact, I never wanted to be in the house. I was blessed to be raised in Southern California, where being outside was as easy as sliding into a pair of swim trunks. Yet that piano became a symbol of my unsung songs as well as the few songs my mother played. They were dark, classic pieces, dirges that suggested discord.

Which leads to the question: with all of these familial compli-
cations, why was I so happy? I ask because my childhood bliss was
bountiful. I was intoxicated by the wonders of the natural world, as
well as the world of books written by sages like Mary Baker Eddy, who
declared, "Divine Love always has met and always will meet every
human need."

I suppose much of this bliss also had to do with physical exhilara-
tion, the pure thrill of being alive. And then came romance.

Father's Flying Dream,
Facing the Chief

Because the Berkeley Hall theater company was a man short, at age fourteen I was asked to play a small part in *The Stingiest Man in Town*, a musical about Scrooge. Next came the English comedy *The Mouse That Roared*, where I got to employ a German accent that elicited great laughter. That was the moment I experienced the enormous satisfaction of making hundreds of people laugh. Angels were kissing me all over. I felt different. I felt present in a way I had never felt present before. I had discovered this gift for wild physical comedy that was always there but not really manifest, at least not in a formal setting. I could always entertain family and friends, but these audience members were strangers I had touched, and having been touched were strangers no longer. That transformation forged my future. Deep down, I knew I'd never be able to hack a regular life. I figured I was born to act, not because I recognized my budding talent, but because it seemed easy and simple and a good way to get the girls.

The other thing that inspired me, the cause of my original love of acting, was Marlon Brando. He was everything. He was an artist and acting was his animal, his craft. He purposely chose roles that were impossible for him. He put himself in culturally death-defying situations; he risked embarrassment and injury to try to do something holy and good. He was called to test the medium and try on personalities in such a strange and intense way that, for a moment, you're riding on something otherworldly. For some, that would be too out-there. For Brando, it was natural, giving and risking everything. A concentration of a love potion into one tiny drop. I watched him and knew that in an ancient village where your last name was your vocation, we would have been part of the same family, and it was my duty to grow up and join the family trade. Loving Marlon was a kind of adolescent rebellion. My bond with Brando was based on something more than admiration as an actor. Somehow I understood he was also a poet of and for humanity.

It was a Saturday afternoon and I wanted Dad to take me to the movies. We liked seeing films together.

"What do you want to see?" he asked.

"*The Godfather.*"

"Anything but that."

"Why?" I asked. "Everyone says it's great."

"Too violent."

My first paying role was a commercial for cheeseburgers. I was probably thirteen. Through a friend's dad who managed the Osmonds, I was hired by an ad agency for a national TV spot. The director liked my look and gave me the few lines that had to be memorized. The main job was to act like I was enjoying gobbling up the burger. Problem was, I wasn't. The thing tasted like cardboard. The director kept telling me to put my heart into it. I couldn't. I didn't. I walked off the set and never appeared in the commercial and never got paid, my first act of artistic integrity.

Onstage, I felt at home and also not at home. That contradiction was not unpleasant. I had some innate confidence that I could turn myself into a character. In my earliest acting experiences, I saw this contradiction cropping up everywhere. I was and was not the character I played. The character went through me, and therefore was me, even as I went through the character and became him. Pieces of me and pieces of him merged. I'm articulating now something I couldn't articulate then, but it was something I deeply felt. The excitement was extraordinary. For the rest of my life, I would be fascinated by the process of leaving myself to find a character who inevitably contained elements of myself. I was losing myself and finding myself at the same time.

I jump ahead decades to a Comic-Con convention where Batman fans were eager for autographs. I always appreciate their enthusiasm. Fans donned the costumes of their screen heroes and heroines, generating adrenaline-fueled overheated mayhem. In the midst of this pop culture fury, a Native American with long braids walked up to me, looked me straight in the eye, and said, "What is the nature of acting?"

I was prepared for the question. The answer came in the form of a recurring dream—not a dream of my own but a dream of my father's that he had relayed to me. I, in turn, relayed it to my questioner: A Native American chief, looking perhaps not unlike the man standing before me, furiously ran after Dad, threatening him with a tomahawk. It only makes sense that my father, in his depths of sleep, was reliving the true story of his own father being similarly attacked. In the dream, when Dad was pursued all the way to the edge of a cliff, he jumped toward a sea of water below and then, as he was falling, woke up. Same dream, night after night, until one blessed night my father didn't jump off the cliff but instead turned to his assailant and said, "Okay, just do it. Kill me." But when the Native assailed my father, rather than ruin his flesh, he went right through him, went through his body and his spirit. They became one. And together, they began to fly. That's acting. To inhabit. To be in communion with an invisible force. My new Comic-Con friend nodded. He fully understood.

I have a feeling my father's dream may have been informed by *Little Big Man*, starring Dustin Hoffman. Dad took me to see it when I was ten. Director Arthur Penn translated Thomas Berger's novel into the most arresting Western Hollywood has ever made. That's because the story doesn't shy away from the genocidal sin that sits in the bosom of the American adventure. As a wide-eyed youngster, I took it all in. I've never forgotten the line Little Big Man's adopted grandfather Old Lodge Skins utters to express joy: "My heart soars like a hawk." The film had my heart soaring.

For Dad, raised on John Wayne machismo and Westerns glorifying the slaughter of Native Americans, it was a tough film to watch. He belonged to the school that says real men don't cry. This time, though, I saw he was on the verge of tears. He couldn't go directly to the car and drive home. He and I walked around the block several times while he started telling me stories. Those were my first hints that our ancestry was connected to Native Americans, many of whom, according to Dad, had suffered cruel injustice. My father didn't elaborate. I don't know whether that was because he simply didn't want to conjure up a painful past or because he wasn't in command of the facts. It was all vague, but it really didn't matter. The film deeply affected him.

Hoffman affected me in a much different way when, as a teen, I saw *The Graduate*. I was mesmerized by the end of the film, when Dustin shows up at church, bangs on the glass above the altar, and saves his sweetheart from marrying a man she doesn't love. They escape the predictable world of middle-class conformity and head out into a new world of unpredictable romance. There came a glorious moment when, as an adult, I got to tell Dustin how he had inspired me. Those two roles came around at just the right time. I loved him as an adopted Native American and loved him just as much as a projection of a young man willing to do whatever it took to live for love, even running off to points unknown. Man, did I relate!

Spooked by Love

I was covered in wanderlust.

I wandered not only into nature; I wandered between the homes of Mom and Dad, seeking solace that was never quite there. My parents' separation was a setup for deceit. I could tell Mom I was at Dad's and vice versa. Because they had no interest in speaking to one another, I was free to roam.

Roaming through Chatsworth had its limits. I could only go so far and see so much. No matter how spread out, suburbia imposes stultifying confinement. That may be another reason why my roaming took a literary bent. Books have no such confinement. They opened me to the world. I read everyone from Thomas Mann to Edgar Allan Poe.

To live inside a book was one thing, but to act inside a play was a far more visceral thrill. There the paradox of lost-and-found was irresistible. Lose Chatsworth, find Elizabethan England. Find Shakespeare. And having found Shakespeare, never look back.

That this happened to me was the result of pure luck. At fourteen, I left Berkeley Hall and enrolled at Chatsworth High. The next year I received a learner's permit, allowing me to flee to the desert on weekends. My first car was a sky-blue Mercedes 280SL, bought for me when my father was flush. I promised I'd pay him back. It took me years, but eventually I did. The Benz was heaven. I raced that car with many fools on Interstate 405. I went wherever my parents weren't, up and down the California coast, emulating the plays of Sam Shepard, a man who, later in life, would be a friend and fellow rabble-rouser. Even before digesting the work of Kerouac and Ginsberg, I lived as a beatnik. I was writing plays and poems, aware that my family history is replete with scribes of every stripe, from troubadours to historians.

At a ridiculously early age, I was spiritually ambitious, devising five-year plans to achieve self-realization and change my life forever. I'm convinced that every plan worked, even as every plan failed. I carried heavy books on my outings into nature. When they became too heavy to lug any longer, I left them at my favorite sights, imagining that a fellow wanderer would find enlightenment at the very spot where I had laid my burden down.

Brother Wesley was far more product oriented than me. During our Arizona summers with Mom, he wrote plays and films, and having rehearsed us into the ground, he achieved a level of artistry you might imagine from a childhood Steven Spielberg. Once he gathered up every wire coat hanger in the house to twist into a mammoth octopus for his adaptation of *20,000 Leagues Under the Sea*. Wesley's imagination dwarfed mine, even with my penchant for absurdity. His range of talents was staggering.

I am reminded of an unforgettable on-screen brotherhood, one of the few moments in my career reminiscent of the innocent and gnarly rapture of my boyhood. If you listen closely to certain scenes in *Kiss Kiss Bang Bang*, you can hear me trying to mess with Robert Downey Jr., even as the cameras were rolling. You can hear him saying, "Val, seriously, stop. Shut up, Val." Oh man, I could watch those scenes over and over. Robert is a brother to me and one of the few creatures who reminds me of Wesley's feral, incomparable spirit.

Anyway, Wes would make these plays or films and proudly introduce them to the after-dinner guests assembled in the lobby of Mom and Bill's ranch. By that time, though, Bill was already crocked and couldn't restrain from shouting out the blue jokes he'd just read in the current *Playboy*. We cringed but carried on. Fortunately–and miraculously–Bill ultimately had a healing from hooch.

In the seventies, Beverly Hills High was seen as the ultimate site for student actors–everyone from Carrie Fisher to Jamie Lee Curtis to Nic Cage–and I did spend time in that enclave of affluence. But Beverly Hills gave me no pleasure and in fact added to my antipathy for the Westside of Los Angeles. With all this wealth, why no city planning? Why no architectural cohesion? The place was a mad urban scramble, an ugly maze best described back in the sixties by Burt Bacharach and Hal David when they had Dionne Warwick singing, "LA is a great big freeway."

Fortunately–and amazingly–Chatsworth's drama department was ranked second only to that of Beverly Hills High. The staff included a brilliant instructor, Robert Carrelli, the kind of drama teacher who changes lives. At Chatsworth, a few budding actors stood out, one of whom was Mare Winningham. She was grounded and so wise beyond her years, an incredible talent. And she became my first real girlfriend. I felt so much less worldly and glamorous. And yet, no doubt about it, Mare and I fell in love. When Mare and I were cast in shows together, it ignited some kind of crazy competitive streak, equally fierce in each of us. Backstage we would bicker like divorcés. If anything, that might have energized our acting. The third member of our friendship trio was Wesley's close friend Brad Koepenick, who would later transition

With Mare Winningham and awards won at the
Los Angeles Valley College Play Festival

from underage dangler-on to talented actor with dazzling wit. Brad became a calming presence and an integral ingredient to life for both me
and Mare, as he remains today. Mare's mother, an English teacher, was
a devout Catholic. I always wondered if she saw my spiritual leanings
as legitimate. She herself had the enlightened aura of a nun. Mare's
dad was considered the best sports coach in the county. Mare had
a lovely older sister and younger brother who turned me on to the
Kinks. Loved their lyrics, although my deeper love was for Led Zep
and Creedence Clearwater and ethereal singer-songwriter Harry Nilsson. And of course the beastly Beatles. Mare is a natural-born singer
with a Judy Garland-like musical presence who sounded more like
Joni Mitchell. She is a sublime soul. To the Winninghams, I was the
boy they feared would impair Mare's otherwise impeccable reputation. (I'm paraphrasing here.) They thought I was out to ruin her life.
I didn't mean to, but they were right. Nonetheless, Mare became my

I, Val Kilmer 4/02/7?
will indeed and
hitherto agree to,
if in fact I do not
place at the upcoming
Shakespeare Festival
on the date of April 23,
In the year of our lord
nineteen hundred and
seventy seven, wash
your new car at least
once a week, until the
time I depart for the
Big Apple. Signed by Kilmer
BOY GENIUS

A note to drama teacher Robert Carelli upon deciding at the last minute to change my monologue for a competition: "I, Val Kilmer, will indeed and hitherto agree to, if in fact I do not place at the upcoming Shakespeare Festival on the date of April 23, in the year of our lord, nineteen hundred and seventy seven, wash your new car at least once a week, until I depart for the Big Apple." I won first place.

With Mare Winningham
in New York City

sweetheart. I was smitten. She and I worked feverishly on weekends, washing cars and doing every other odd job to save money to fly to New York to see genuine Broadway theater.

I'd been to the city once before. A couple years earlier I went to Pittsburgh, where stepdad Bill had inherited a home from his father. I convinced Mom and Bill to extend our trip to New York. I had to see Gotham. I also had to see Rip Torn playing the son in *The Glass Menagerie*, because in our school production I'd just played that same part–Tom Wingfield, warehouse worker who dreams of being a poet. I embraced those dreams. Like Tom, I even took up smoking, so I could render the character more realistically. Though I hated the habit, I stayed shackled to cigarettes for a long while. I wasn't a bad Tom, but Torn showed me the difference between good and great. He breathed Tom's very breath.

Like a hundred million first-timers before me, New York fueled my fires. I ran with its rhythms. Its energy had me crazy. I quote from Steely Dan's "Green Book," which half-quotes Burt Lancaster's sleazy gossip king in *Sweet Smell of Success*: "I'm so in love with this dirty city, its crazy grid of desire." I promised Broadway I'd be back.

I kept the promise when Mare and I arrived with our school drama group. Our Times Square hotel was dormlike, with boys and girls in separate rooms, but, resourceful teenagers that we were, Mare and I found a way to snuggle in the hallway. At one point we slept most of the night there. Utter bliss. We took a chance on love.

While I was going with Mare, I certainly kissed other girls but never imagined she would kiss another boy until I had an extraordinary dream. It happened when I was visiting my mom in Arizona. In the vision, I saw Mare with another boy in Idyllwild, some four hours away at the foot of the San Jacinto Mountains. When I awoke, I borrowed my stepdad's car and drove three hundred miles. When I arrived, I followed some signs that pointed to a swimming club. I saw a white arrow etched in a tree. I was moving by feel and feel alone. Then, just as in my dream, coming out of the dark woods, I saw Mare and this boy kissing. I was angry and hurt but, more than anything, amazed at the accuracy of my premonition. I was spooked by love.

The Deepest Wound

Back in Chatsworth, Mare and I ended our romance but continued our friendship. We both grew increasingly enamored of theater. We came up in an era when school drama productions were huge. Some of our performances were reviewed in the *Los Angeles Times*. When the school put on *The Sound of Music*, Mare played Maria. Bit by the classical bug, I acted in Chekhov's *Uncle Vanya*, *Equus*, *The Prime of Miss Jean Brodie*, *Henry IV*, *Richard II*, and *Macbeth*. The sophistication of our repertoire was phenomenal.

What does it mean to be called a ham? Was I a ham? I was naturally and inordinately theatrical. I liked to carry on. I liked attention. I liked extravagant speech. I liked to emote. I liked to talk. It didn't matter that I usually didn't know what I was talking about. And I loved it when dramatists elevated talk to poetry. So I did the same. I started writing dramas and poems. Some might have been painfully bad, but some might have shown signs of promise.

The Hollywood Professional School, where I enrolled for a year, was filled with hams, kids hungry to stand before audiences and elicit a positive response. I wound up there because some friends from grade school had told me about it. They had formed a singing duo and were often on the road. They said the school didn't care and the teachers didn't keep track of who played hooky. They said so many of the kids were either out on auditions or in rehearsal that attendance records were loose, and you could show up or skip school whenever you wanted—a system that suited me fine.

Hollywood in the midseventies was filled with ghosts. Jimi Hendrix, Janis Joplin, and Jim Morrison had died only a few years earlier, and the last remnants of hippiedom were on full display: wild-eyed girls who, lost from their last acid trip, never found their way home; homeless vagrants; homeless musicians; porn shops; sleazy lingerie boutiques. It was tough telling the down-and-out homeless from the down-and-out musicians. Behind the anonymous doors of recording studios, Earth, Wind & Fire was cutting "Shining Star," Glen Campbell was singing "Rhinestone Cowboy," and Stevie Wonder was putting the final touches on *Songs in the Key of Life*. But I was just a kid standing in front of the window of Frederick's of Hollywood mystified by the peekaboo brassieres and panties sculpted in scarlet and hot pink. Hollywood was seedy, but sensationally so. Like its New York City counterpart, Times Square, it would ultimately be sanitized in the name of wholesome family tourism, but I liked danger lurking around the corner. The man who dressed in tatters and couldn't stop muttering obscenities to himself didn't bother me. I'd started reading the poet Charles Bukowski, who wrote, "Some people never go crazy. What truly horrible lives they must lead."

I always wanted to get out of Los Angeles. I saw it as a sunscorched city whose mission was to please the world at any cost so that the world, in turn, would reward its roster of outrageous heroes

with ridiculous wealth. If Hollywood was all about harmless entertainment, Manhattan was about harmful art. I saw New York City as
dangerous and daring. New York City was the country's center of classical theater. I gravitated toward that genre—with its bloody and murderous themes—because it was the hardest to master.

One meaningful morning I happened to mention to brother Mark
something about acting schools. I was debating between the Royal
Academy of Dramatic Art and THE Juilliard School. (The capitalization
is intentional for reasons you'll discover shortly.) I was thinking ahead.
Mark had an interesting response. "You're trying to decide between
fancy drama schools that will seal your fate in the history of theater
while I'm trying to decide between Bob's Big Boy and Burger King.
What are you?"

"The only thing I can ever be: an actor."

So off I went to the city where Brando, the north star of my theatrical fantasies, had lit up the night thirty-three years earlier.

On the way to New York, Mom, Bill, and I stopped at Bill's house
in Pittsburgh. In the past, I'd stay in the same room with my brothers. But Mark was enrolled in a Christian Science college, and Wesley
was about to start Chatsworth High. It was September. It was hot and
humid. I wasn't used to humidity. Finally I was able to fall asleep. Even
now, I can remember the details of my dream. I was having an easy
discussion with Mare and her mom about God. I asked Mrs. Winningham if she was afraid of death. She answered instantly. "No, not at
all," she said. "Because I'll be with my creator. I look forward to meeting whoever/whatever created me." I said, "Thank you for describing
death in this way. You make me feel comfortable." I awoke from the
dream to the sound of a ringing phone. Afraid it would awaken Mom,
I ran to answer it. It was Mark. He asked, "Where are you?" I knew. "In

the kitchen," I said. He told me to go downstairs and call him back. I did. He said that our little brother, Wesley, had suffered an epileptic fit in the Jacuzzi, drowned, and died in the ambulance. I paused. I breathed.

I remember trying to comfort Mark, saying that it was impossible for Wesley to be gone since life is eternal and all of us are here forever. Mark listened and then said, "Put Mom on the phone." Mom fell apart, as did Bill. Wesley was Bill's favorite. Wesley was everyone's favorite. The adults wept like children. Yet the adults, being adults, knew they had to make plans. We would not be driving on to New York. We would be flying home to bury my brother.

And as for my dad, everything that was rapid and rapturous about him slowed almost to a halt. His charisma faded. The house went from fantastical, filled with friends and frenetic energy, to almost completely abandoned.

I felt abandoned. I didn't even want to view his body. He had been so full of life; I couldn't understand why anyone would want to see him not breathing. I avoided craziness only because of my faith. My faith fortified me. I leaned on the teachings of Mrs. Eddy, who understood God only in terms of positivity. At the same time, this became *the* tragic event of my young life. Perhaps my entire life. Wesley's death changed everything. I tried to accept the idea, substantiated by reading the Bard, that tragedy is not without its gifts. But acceptance was and will always be onerous. As I write these words, I yearn for Wesley's company. I want my brother alive, physically not just spiritually. I want him back. I want him standing next to me. I understand this is selfish. Sometimes he comes to me through other talents—talented people, male and female—and he kind of chastises me for being silly about life. I apologize and he says, "Even that is a form of selfishness. Just get on with it. No one wants to see or hear a handsome, successful, talented writer-actor-director who gets the most impossible-to-get girls in the world complain about a damn thing. Plus, all that is nothing. Nothing compared to your real purpose. Your gift of healing. That's why you are here and that's why you will stay. Get healing, ya wuss. Get on with it."

SAND

[THE SET IS BARE. AN ACTOR LAYS ON HIS SIDE, SLIGHTLY
PROPPED UP.]

Act and ye shall receive
It lives green from the desert
For the desert believes
Sand, it is poured in my side
When it is still, and it is night,
And ground on even lines rests
In sleep.
When sheets and pillows and smooth mounds that
Comfort are like home-safe, distort to move in
To what is pain for me . . . then I move, and then I ask
For my dream again.

[THE ACTOR SITS UP, AS IF HE HAS BEEN TAKEN OUT OF
CHARACTER. LOOKS DIRECTLY INTO SOME MEMBERS OF THE
HOUSE AS IF THEY ARE IN CHARGE OF HIS FATE.]

[HUMBLY] I'm sorry. Can I start over?

[IF THERE IS A RESPONSE, HE ABRUPTLY CHANGES, ALMOST
SNIDELY, BUT WITH DEEP COMPASSION, ALMOST SADLY. AS IF
THERE IS NOW NO WAY OUT FOR ANY OF US, EVER.]

No. And that's a point, for I can never really be sorry.
I can only apologize for you . . .

For you she said, [AT GREAT COST] "It is plain that nothing can be added
To the mind already full . . ."
Now I truly believe that; only it must be as when
(In our ignorance of innocence)
We had our choice of things, because we left things

The way they are.
Without sand. It is poured in my side, when it is still
And it is night
And I see plain
And my error remains
And I choose, to lose my senses,
To sand . . . [APPEALING TO THE EVER-PRESENT DIVINE PRESENCE]
Again?

—Wickenburg, Arizona, 1976

THE Juilliard School

There was no turning back from New York. I went there shortly after Wesley's funeral. I needed it, wanted it, was incapable of resisting. The audition required two readings—one classical, one contemporary. For the classical, I chose Mercutio's soliloquy on Queen Mab, the fabulous doyenne of the faeries whom Shakespeare transforms into a hag. For the contemporary selection, I announced that I would be reading my own poem, "Sand."

They loved it. One examiner called my poem a psalm. Another said it felt like I was auditioning them rather than vice versa. That's what I was going for. They also liked the fact that I had written a play. Either way, the merciful gods granted me admission. As a sixteen-year-old high school dropout, I became the youngest kid ever accepted to their drama school.

Mare didn't want to go to theater school. There wasn't anywhere for her to go that could help her put together the few last threads of her wedding dress of success she had been hand-stitching since was four or five. She was Bob Dylan-alive, wanted to share it right now.

Although THE Juilliard would have welcomed her, she went straight to Hollywood, and within two years, she won an Emmy.

From the moment I stepped on campus, I was skeptical. The name itself bothered me. You were instructed to say THE Juilliard School. You could not omit the THE. My attitude was, to hell with the THE. A school's A school. Just as there isn't THE truth; there's A truth. My little brother was just taken away and I, too, had some Bob Dylan-now in me—in my naked now.

Opening day was brutal. It didn't help to be told that one of the people sitting next to us wouldn't be there next year. What was this—the marines? It was suggested that of the thirty or so kids in this new class, only half would survive. What would be our ruin? When I asked the question, I was told lack of focus, an inadequate work ethic, and insufficient intellect. Then why were we there to begin with? These instructors couldn't allow us the innocent delight of initiation without piling on a heaping serving of dread.

Fear, not Love, was the introductory lesson. Fear of not measuring up. Fear of being dropped. Fear of displeasing the maestros. The mentality was boot camp. Tear the little bastards apart and build them back up. You think you can speak Shakespeare's iambic pentameter—well, you can't. Let us make it plain. You do not know how to talk. You do not know how to walk. You do not know how to think. You do not know how to listen. Or laugh. Or cry. Or read Konstantin Stanislavski with even a minimum of comprehension.

I filled my room on campus with abstract paintings by myself and Wesley to stay humble and inspired and strange. I wrote and drew and resisted a classical approach and a one-sided career. Art was art. And it certainly wasn't this or that. It was all of it. I would tell my classmates, "We're paying a truckload of money for tuition. We're working as waiters to make ends meet, and these puritans are using army

Training in a Suzuki Method class at THE Juilliard School, 1981

training to crush our spirit. Don't listen to them. They can't teach be-cause they don't know how to love. Let's make up our own class. Let's find the Love in this work."

The question, then, is this: how in hell did I survive four years at THE Juilliard? The answer is that I became A rebel. With a cause. Sometimes quietly, sometimes provokingly loud. I was just a kid devel-oping my style. My cause was to survive the academy and, with some subversive flair, use it to get me into the real world of theater. I knew damn well it was a jumping-off point. It also didn't help that my father, although he covered my college tuition, liked to manipulate me with money. He paid the rent for my small apartment overlooking Central Park but used that fact to lord over me. When he was displeased with me, he'd stop paying the rent. I'd call and ask why. He'd say that if I didn't call more often, it wasn't fair. During the coldest New York winter in seventy years, he ignored my utility bills. The city cut off the heat and I contracted pneumonia. After two years of this folly, I said to hell with him. One of the reasons I had left California for New York was to escape my father. He knew that and pushed back. I saw that I had to push back even more. So I stopped taking his money. Instead I asked my stepdad for a loan that I was able to pay back once I was out in the working world of New York theater.

First thing we did at THE Juilliard was *Richard III*. Our teachers called it a "discovery play." We were supposed to discover ourselves in the play. It should have been called a "discover-how-you'll-fall-on-your-ass play." Yet I tackled it, principally because I was cast as Richard. I liked leads. What actor doesn't? Especially a chance to play a hunchbacked, demented, scheming, evil monarch who opens the play with that most ominous of lines: "Now is the winter of our discontent."

I felt like Popeye gobbling down spinach. I gorged on that fiery iambic pentameter and found a superpower. So much so that in the second scene, after saying to a soldier, "Unmanner'd dog!" I took my poor classmate by his costume, a burlap sack, and flung him into the wall of the rehearsal space. Like a cartoon character, he flew right through it, as if it were paper. Well . . . if that wasn't a crowd pleaser! Fortunately, the actor wasn't harmed. In fact, he loved it. He was stuck on the other side of the wall, with just his arms and legs hanging through. We tried to gracefully pull him back through and stay on cue. He was a soldier, one of my boys for the pending war with THE Juilliard School. I loved being hateful Richard. Loved his unmerciful contempt for his physical disfigurement, loved how he declaims, "I, that am rudely stamp'd." In other words, he hates his looks and uses his fury to steal the crown. To do so, he must seduce Lady Anne, despite the fact that Richard has killed her dad and husband. Gaining her favor requires extreme histrionics. He takes a sword and offers to kill himself, then gives the sword to Anne so she might kill him. All this to prove his repentance. I coaxed the girl playing Anne nearly to impale me.

At one point I broke character, and when Anne turned away from my boyish flirting, I quickly made a repulsive face. The audience howled. I did all kinds of schtick. The schtick paid off—for Richard and for me. Richard gets the girl and the crown and, in a triumphant monologue, asks, "Was ever woman in this humour woo'd? / Was ever woman in this humour won?"

I myself felt triumphant. Now I'm going to say something that sounds self-serving because it *is* self-serving. But it's also the truth. I never played a leading role at THE Juilliard without receiving a standing ovation. I was a teenage actor on fire. Part of that fire was fueled by my animosity for the academy. I was dead set on showing how I could woo and win the audience while ignoring academic techniques.

What were those techniques? Or is *technique* even the right word?

I struggle to explain my methodology. I don't put myself in the same class as Bob Dylan, but I have a feeling if you asked him to explain his methodology of writing or singing songs, he'd simply say, "I just do it." That four-word explanation, as simplistic as it might sound, suits me fine. Or as Marlon used to say in a myriad of different ways—though my favorite was always the simplest—"Fill yourself up with all the character's magic stuff, spin it up, then *let fly!*" When it comes to acting, I just do it. Those four words could be expanded into four thousand or four hundred thousand. But I'm not sure the expansion would shed much light.

Actually those four words could be too many. You could cut them in half and say to act is simply *to be*. If Hamlet is the ultimate role and if "To be or not to be" the ultimate question, then the ultimate answer is yes. Be. It's actually the same answer God gives when asked to describe his nature: "I am." That's it. God has always been my comfort, and Hamlet has always been my man.

Even as a know-nothing youth, I knew how to pray for direction against the faculty's orthodox dictums. Praying is unifying oneself with life's purpose. I quote Mary Baker Eddy, "To live so as to keep human consciousness in constant relationship to the divine, the spiritual and the eternal is to individualize infinite spirit, and this is Christian Science." And if the words *Christian Science* grate on you, may I suggest you substitute the words *divine Love*. I don't think KRS-ONE or any great poet gets too hung up on meanings if they are caught up in the spirit, in the moment of inspiration. Mrs. Eddy wrote that *Science* and *Christian* were the two most important words in the English language. I have spent over half my life pondering alternatives to those words, attempting to find two that are equally important. This is not the subject of this chapter or even this book. I am merely attempting to give you an idea of what kind of rabbit hole we were invited or demanded to jump into in our first year at THE Juilliard School. I don't want to sound pompous or pretentious, but that was my way, even as a teen actor: I was motivated by Love's purpose. Love said love Richard III. Understand Richard III. Rely on divine principle to see how this desperately unhappy king was able to drain all humanity from his soul. Focus on his drained soul for ten seconds or ten minutes or ten hours. Let go of ideas. Focus on color. Focus on sound without ideas. Let go of everything and sink onto the floor. Maybe lie down and sleep on the floor for a half hour. You wouldn't believe how I got screamed at for sleeping on the stage floor before rehearsals.

"What are you doing, Val?"

"Why are you goofing off, Val?"

"Why are you asleep at the very moment you need to be awake?"

I had no answers. To tell them I was simply yielding would not have assuaged their anger. I let them be angry. I continued to sleep.

When I awoke, often something was there—an understanding I had previously lacked. Mind you, I was never opposed to rehearsal. I liked it. I accepted the notion that craft is endless repetition. It's finding joy in the smallest gesture. The cat cleans itself with its left foot folded over and repeats the motion fifty times. I can be the cat. I can clean myself. I can practice. I can repeat. I abandon my old conscience and find the new conscience that makes Hamlet a coward. I can be that coward. All this is to say that in the context of an academy dedicated to its own sort of orthodoxy, I learned that the theater of the absurd was more than a genre. The theater has always been an arena of the absurd, whether the classical theater of Shakespeare and Molière or the modern theater of Chekhov and Ibsen. The avant-garde absurdists—Beckett, Genet, Pinter—carried on the tradition. The tradition is a theatrical reflection of life, and the reflection, at least as far as I can see, is always skewed.

I was blessed to always take it seriously and not seriously at all. Seriously because, as Hamlet said, we may always be on the verge of shuffling off this mortal coil. And that's a serious thing. But not seriously because, in following *perfect man*—Willie Nelson's term for Christ—we know we'll never achieve that status. If we seriously think that we will, we confuse ourselves with God. Our seriousness will do us in. That's another reason I've always loved the wildly comic theatrical dance.

That's the dance I began as a teenage actor. Serious and silly at the same time. Sane and insane at the same time. Allowing myself to travel the distance between eagerness and hesitancy. Willing and unwilling. Teachable and unteachable. Pliable and stubborn. Ready and reluctant. Driven by an inherent need for attention—wherever that need might come from—and tempered by a skepticism of traditional methods to gain such attention.

All we have as artists is our instincts, to begin with.

Tadashi Suzuki and the
Elusive Nature of Fate

I am suddenly aware of how, in writing a memoir like this, I can get riled up. Just a few pages back, I was on a tirade, bemoaning the stilted academic ambience of THE Juilliard. I fancy myself a rebel, so at any opportunity, I'll go off. Hear me roar. Well, I like rebelling and I like roaring, but in this enterprise I'm committed to reflection. I had amazing teachers and directors that made THE Juilliard School THE best school in the world. And I'll say THE with pride till the day I die.

The truth is that when I got to THE Juilliard, I had a terribly strong Californian accent, which was only to be replaced by a proper general American kind of transatlantic theater-snob accent. But the godly vocal coach at school, Tim Monich, helped me work my voice like it was a trumpet. He is a master of his craft, also from the West Coast, and a dutiful disciple of the mighty Edith Skinner, whom we had the extreme privilege of studying with in her last years. Tim got me. He was patient, but he gave it to you straight. I vowed to never take a project without him. You'd be shocked at how many directors and producers wouldn't allow me to bring him on. In so many ways theater is more earnest than film, and I miss it and love it so much.

Which brings me to someone I can't forget: Michael Langham, the drama director at THE Juilliard School. Born in England in 1919, Langham fought for the British Army in World War II and spent five years in German prisoner-of-war camps. I'd heard it was in these camps that he honed his theater skills, directing plays among the prisoners. I'd try to get him to talk about it. He never would. He was a gentle, loving man, and we were more than lucky to have him around. He talked *to* students. Another teacher at THE Juilliard, Alan Schneider, was a pillar of American theater, having directed the American premieres of many Beckett plays including *Waiting for Godot*, but he talked *at* us. Big difference. True teachers are givers, and Langham gave all. In his dry manner, he gave Love. He recognized my talent and candor and would call me into his office, wanting to know whether there were any demons among his instructors. I named a few, and I'm convinced he took those few to task. He saw the drawbacks of THE Juilliard School's rigidity and did his best to loosen things up. But schools are cultures with long histories not easily altered. Michael Langham was a selfless man who did all he could to promote a humane pedagogy.

Things got a little happier at THE Juilliard School when we did Chekhov's *The Wood Demon*, an earlier working of *Uncle Vanya*. *Uncle Vanya* is brilliant. *The Wood Demon* ain't, but it made me appreciate how, by staying true to his craft, the playwright went from the mediocre to the marvelous. It also gave me a chance to advocate for greater equality in our casting, as I insisted the role of my co-lead go to an African American classmate.

Even more interesting than *The Wood Demon* was my plan for a

Performing *Orestes* with fellow student Mary Johnson
at THE Juilliard School, 1981

play about a nefarious character. It was a collective effort I cowrote with my Juilliard classmates, *How It All Began*. The project would not have happened without the support of Michael Langham, who encouraged experimental writing. My own attitude was, then and now, unrelentingly proactive. If the material was not there, I'd write it. I relished the idea of writing as a group. I saw it as jazz. Let everyone jam. I unapologetically took the lead: as Michael Baumann—the play was based on his memoir—a man who went from protester to terrorist and then figured out through his newfound religion, rock and roll, that you can't take away a gun with a gun. The moral of the story was that no matter where we look, whether to Malcolm X or Rudi Dutschke or John Lennon, Love conquers hate in the most unflinching way. We mounted it with the generosity of a hot young director named Des McAnuff.

Great opening night—so great, in fact, that renowned producer and director Joseph Papp saw it and convinced THE Juilliard School to put more money into the production. We worked on it all through our third year and then throughout the summer and all through our fourth year. We had it so tight. I graduated on a Friday and on Monday we were doing a tech rehearsal at Papp's prestigious Public Theater. Papp wasn't the classiest or the wealthiest or the most well-read, but he created theater for the people. He had a decades-long history of doing it right, workshopping young, emerging talent with seasoned, beloved directors and writers. Joe rubbed sticks together and made fire. The first was a little musical simply called *Hair*. The second was a more experimental, behind-the-scenes concept. It would come to be called *A Chorus Line*.

How It All Began ran for six weeks. The reviews were raves. I was suddenly a pro. But somewhere along the way our monologues grew longer, the play stretched from ninety minutes to more than two hours, and the air went out of the balloon. Arrogance did us in. Or at least did me in.

I felt the power before I had it. It was from the universe, or it was from my soul. I was about to become one of the youngest stars on Broadway, but as I looked deep inside myself, I felt I wasn't ready for the honor. Some might have said I was running away from my destiny, and at least one part of that would always be true. I was running. Perhaps I should have hung out and at least gambled a bit with the Icarus myth and tested the strength of the foundation all those amazing teachers and directors and fellow actors had given me. It was so easy though. They just handed it to me, and it was a golden door to the Great White Way. Joe Papp solidified what was a quiet whisper throughout all the in-the-know hipsters of the new American theater, as well as the established classical theater crowd, all eighty-seven of them. It was the hardest work around.

I went to see every Broadway hit time would allow, and sometimes didn't allow. The world of working theater is rarefied air, and there aren't that many who stick it out.

I saw Sam Shepard's *True West* with John Malkovich and Gary Sinise more times than I could count. It was a master class. Theater like that is worth selling your best boots or your wedding ring to see, because it's priceless and then it's gone. You can buy another ring. But you can't go back in time. I remember being so moved that I grew shy. I was so confident in my own play but too nervous to go backstage and sit at Malkovich's feet. Why? Maybe he would've liked a mentee.

Now that I think about it, it was probably a big mistake. It would have been such a meaningful life, though a far less glittery one. Being a really great theater actor didn't mean you could necessarily afford a comfortable home or health insurance. I knew actors who had

Tonys and lived off bodega bagels, eggs, and cheese. And it started to depress me.

After graduating from THE Juilliard School, I was given two golden opportunities. The first came from my Christian Science practitioner. While in drama school, I continued to attend services. My faith did not flag. I felt the spirit as tangibly as I felt the spring breeze blowing off the Hudson. This practitioner was an elderly woman who had been in vaudeville and found success as an actor before giving up *la vida loca* for truth and grounding. When it came to ministry, she was the real thing. She had the gift of healing. She said that I too possessed that gift and asked me to accept a role as her acolyte and eventually her replacement. She quoted Mrs. Eddy: "To live and let live, without clamor for distinction or recognition; to wait on divine Love; to write truth first on the tablet of one's own heart—this is the sanity and perfection of living." I could have stayed. I could have lived a patient life. An earnest life. An experience on earth defined by divine healing.

Like Moses, I said no. I said I didn't want the job. In essence, I believe I said no to the Fates because, unlike Moses, I would never pick up the staff. To this day I wonder whether I denied my destiny. Or should I say, I was pretty damn sure I was running away from my destiny.

I was just very, very scared.

The second opportunity came a little later from Tadashi Suzuki, considered the Japanese Stanislavski. He headed the Suzuki Company of Toga. His reputation was that of an intense and rigorous director and maestro. I read that when his workshops were over, the participants were dripping in sweat and on the verge of collapse. I had met his lead actor, a Japanese-Chinese woman. Watching her perform, I was spellbound. She was Brando. She was on that level. She took

Tadashi Suzuki

acting to a place of sublimity I had never known existed. She also saw me perform at THE Juilliard School. Each year she and Suzuki offered two Americans the chance to study at Toga. I was chosen. I could have gone. Learned a whole new method. Immersed myself in a whole new culture. And gone on to star in obscure plays for the rest of my life. I would have had a modest but comfortable income. And lead the life of a pure artist. Again, I ran away from destiny, this time passing up the chance to study with Suzuki to instead live with Cher atop Caesars Palace in Las Vegas, Nevada.

Cher Likes My Harley

I was sitting alone in a mid-Manhattan restaurant eating pasta when a lady friend came up and said, "Someone is interested in meeting you."

"Who?"

"Cher."

Well, if it had been 1960 and that word had been *Bardot*, I would have jumped out of my seat. But Cher was different. Her name shocked me to the point that I spit out my spaghetti while exclaiming, "No!"

I saw Cher as a less-than-fascinating character out of the gossip rags. I was not motivated to meet her, not out of snobbery but simply because I was sure we had nothing in common.

"Our conversation wouldn't last more than three minutes," I said.

"You don't know her," said our friend.

"True. But why are you pushing so hard?"

"Her real personality is different than her TV personality. I guarantee, she's the funniest person you'll ever meet."

Because our friend was nearly frantic to facilitate the encounter, I conceded. It happened on another night in another restaurant where there must have been ten people at the table. I'd been told that if I did not find Cher compelling, I could leave. I stayed. Cher was funny, hysterically funny. I ended up driving her home on the back of my Harley through the streets of Manhattan. She loved the Harley. We both loved laughing and went on doing so for well over a year. At the same time, to perfect her teeth, she was wearing braces. I joked that they gave her the look of her emotional age: fourteen. I used to tell her when she turned sixteen I would buy her a Porsche.

Cher was living in New York, where she was pursuing an acting career that got off to a roaring start with *Come Back to the Five and Dime, Jimmy Dean, Jimmy Dean*, directed for both Broadway and film by Robert Altman. Cher was—and is, and will always be—formidable. The year we met I was twenty-one, and Cher, then in her midthirties, looked even younger than I did. She chastised me for constantly carrying around a copy of *Ulysses* as if it were a purse, a move she thought was pretentious if not horrifyingly nerdy. I was nonetheless smitten (and flattered and aroused and exhilarated) to be with so glamorous a star who had dated men as diverse as David Geffen and Gregg Allman. After her successful run on Broadway, her intention was to return to California. She wanted me to go back with her. I wasn't eager to leave the stage, and this was the moment when Tadashi Suzuki offered me a chance to study with him. It was a difficult decision. Or was it? Maybe I want to call the decision difficult in order to sound more profound. Maybe the decision to leave New York and go to Hollywood with Cher was actually easy.

Post-THE Juilliard School, New York had been easy. I had been certain that my big Broadway break would be *Slab Boys*, the work of John Byrne, a Scotsman who wrote a gripping autobiographical reflection of his experience in a carpet plant where working-class boys are looking to escape the tedium of their labor. The two leads are restless youths

With Sean Penn and Kevin Bacon in *Slab Boys*, 1983

who worship James Dean and Elvis. The distinguished director, Robert Allan Ackerman, promised me the lead but then asked if I would mind taking the second lead since Kevin Bacon, fresh off *Diner*, was available. Eager to work, eager to shine on Broadway, I agreed. Next thing I knew, Ackerman had another request. Since Sean Penn, fresh off his role as stoned-out surfer Jeff Spicoli in *Fast Times at Ridgemont High*, was also available, would I mind taking the third? Well, of course I minded, but of course I caved. I had no leverage. My character, unlike the cutting-edge sweating-and-swearing tough guys played by Kevin and Sean, was a clean-cut square on his way to a white-collar position. He was the butt of every joke. It was humiliating. Yet I accepted. I was so enamored of appearing on Broadway that I turned down a part offered by Francis Ford Coppola for *The Outsiders*, a role that went to

Matt Dillon or Tom Cruise or Patrick Swayze or Rob Lowe or Emilio Estevez, I can't remember which.

During *Slab Boys*'s run, Kevin Bacon was cool but Sean Penn was boiling hot. I remember Sean got into a couple of fights. He once showed up with a black eye. I had never been in a fight. I had always been able to avoid them. Brando used to show me all the scars on his hands from bar fights. He told me it was a dead end and not to go down that road. But he seemed to be pleased to tell me about that road I was not to go down. He said his dad was a bar fighter, too. I said I knew. He said how, and I said because of how he said it in *Last Tango in Paris*. He said that was perceptive. I said maybe not that perceptive as perhaps I read it in an interview. I honestly couldn't remember but I did remember how convinced I was when in Bertolucci's film he talked about his dad being a "bar fighter, whore f–r."

The whole experience of the play was bittersweet. Great being on Broadway but difficult being relegated to third place. I did discover, though, that I could play the Good Guy. It became part of my artistic arsenal. As time went on, the Good Guy became an archetype that certain directors saw me fulfilling. In future films–I'm thinking of *Thunderheart*, *The Island of Dr. Moreau*, and *The Ghost and the Darkness*–I played an innocent who required a world-weary badass (Sam Shepard in *Thunderheart*, Marlon Brando in *The Island of Dr. Moreau*, and Michael Douglas in *The Ghost and the Darkness*) to shock me into reality.

Which brings up an interesting point. How does a young actor come of age in a reality principally defined by unreality? The theater isn't real. Movies aren't real. They're reflections of reality. They're art, and art means artifice, and artifice is artificial. That doesn't mean that the artificial is superficial. The artificial can be genuine and seem real. But *seem* is different than *is*. The play ends. The movie is over. The actor goes home. But the actor is eager to move from the unreality of one drama to the unreality of another. In other words, the excitement of life onstage rivals life offstage. So to compensate, the actor feels compelled to goose up his offstage life with as much drama as possible. I say this not to rationalize or excuse. I may well have undermined my life several times even if I weren't an actor caught up in unreality. But I *was* an actor, I *am* an actor, and I'd be lying if I said that my perception of reality hasn't largely been defined by an ever-growing hunger for high drama. The best actors are magical people capable of magical thinking whose lives, for better or worse, become a series of magical revelations.

Being with Cher in New York was pure magic. She encouraged my acting. When the run of *Slab Boys* ended and Edmund White, an extraordinary novelist and chron-icler of his times, cast me in his play as a young lover, she was as pleased as I was. After rehearsals Cher would wait for me outside the theater and whisk me away to the movies or dinner or to see a great play.

The main thing I remember about White's play was the illuminating presence of one of my fellow actors, the great David Warrilow. In his memoir *City Boy*, White referred to him as "one of the leading interpreters of Samuel Beckett." And David certainly did open my eyes to Beckett's genius.

David Warrilow performing at the Brooklyn Academy of Music, 1985

But David was also a superb classical actor. In my same pre-Hollywood stage life, David, Patti LuPone, and I did *As You Like It* at the Guthrie during a freezing Minneapolis winter. It was cold out and sold out. David was the absolute epitome of a seasoned Shakespearean actor. Each night I watched him with wonder. He had mastered the mellifluous cadence of Elizabethan speech. Though I played Orlando, the romantic lead, and David played Jaques, a highly cynical malcontent, David's performance stole the show.

We stayed friends. He gave me a first edition of Walt Whitman's *Leaves of Grass*, which, like the work of Twain, became a guiding light. I treasure that book, along with a first edition of Mary Baker Eddy's *Science and Health*, above all others. After *As You Like It* closed, David moved to Paris, where he tested positive for AIDS. I went to see him. The deterioration was horrific. We sat and watched television, a medium he despised. He was fed by a nurse and his speech, once thrillingly inspiring, became infantile. He died at sixty. France honored him as a Chevalier de l'Ordre des Arts et Lettres, one of their highest accolades for a citizen, but it wasn't enough. There should be a statue. There will be one day. David put the art through his body and it became spiritual. His voice, his movement, his courage—he went all the way most of the time. Oh, David . . . I wish you could have enjoyed a longer life and been spared such a painful demise. I wish the world had recognized and rewarded you with the extravagance you merited. I thank the universe that, for those precious few years, I was graced by your company. Great actors are great teachers, and you were both.

In a similar way, for all her frivolity, Cher was a teacher. She taught me that unabashed ambition was not to be judged. It was to be followed. She followed her instincts for show-business survival with such skill, only a fool would have failed to note her techniques. Of course

With Cher at the BAFTA Awards in London, 1984

there was her indisputable talent. Beyond that, there was her talent for knowing exactly the right platform on which to present that talent. That platform was Hollywood. I followed her there and struggled not to judge myself for doing so.

The simple truth is that Cher made the move irresistible. Cher traffics in intoxicating glamour and I, a Valley boy, fell under her spell. Always dressed to the hilt, always aware of where the press would pursue her and how to put herself in the best light, Cher was a consummate pro. She might have been lobbying for a part, she might have been jealous of a new star, or she might have been missing someone she loved. She calculated and celebrated, as charming as she was cunning. Her superstardom survival is remarkable. She is one of those rare artists who, having triumphed in music and film, has created a category of her own. She's as bright a star as we've got.

Being ushered into the Cher world was heady stuff.

I was with her when she found film success. As a mom with extraordinary empathy and soul, she was brilliant in *Mask*. Through her good offices, I myself auditioned for a part in *Mask*, but director Peter Bogdanovich wasn't moved.

I didn't know it, but my own success was around the corner. Which reminds me of a felicitous phrase: *God wants us to walk but the devil sends a limo.*

Top Secret!

A little before Cher triumphed in *Mask*, I was cast in my first film, the starring role of *Top Secret!*, made by the crew of *Airplane!* It was a goofy spoof of spy flicks. That crew—Jim Abrahams and David and Jerry Zucker—had written *The Kentucky Fried Movie*. I was wild for that film. At fifteen, I was a regular at the Kentucky Fried Theater on Pico Boulevard, a block west of 20th Century Fox, where Abrahams and the Zuckers staged evenings of side-splitting sketches. Having spent the past few years on *How It All Began*, I needed a laugh. Their methodology was deceptively simple—nonstop sight gags, a laugh-out-loud line every sixty seconds, a comedic symphony for the senses. *Top Secret!* continued the *Kentucky Fried Movie* and *Airplane!* lineage by setting its story in East Germany, where Nick Rivers, a pretty-boy Ricky Nelson-style rocker, saves the day. I got to play Nick. That meant I got to sing and play guitar.

Back in Chatsworth, when high school musicals were all the rage and Mare Winningham was enjoying rave reviews for her rendition of *The Sound of Music*, I was not inclined to follow in her footsteps. I

On the set of *Top Secret!* with Jim Abrahams, Jim Carter,
David Zucker (*crouched*), and Jerry Zucker

could sing but didn't see singing as my strength. Yes, I loved singing and was fanatical for raucous rock and roll and hot-blooded rhythm and blues, but when it comes to theater, give me the serious roles. Give me the classics.

I spent four months learning the guitar to the point where my fingers were raw. I was hardly Eric Clapton but I wasn't terrible. But because the writers-directors trafficked in perversity, on the first day of shooting they said I should just pretend to play the guitar—just strum it lightly. "Wait a minute," I said, four months and ten raw fingers later, "you don't want me to play it?" They smiled. They had simply wanted to see my expression when I learned that all my work would be in vain.

The film carried the vibe of an Elvis-in-Hawaii movie to Eastern Europe–John le Carré meets *Happy Days*. The whole thing made me happy. I even got to slip in a Cher poster on the wall of my character's prison cell. (Cher loved it.)

Most of the film was shot in Pinewood Studios outside London. I found a flat in the city, and as I got situated I phoned reception at the local Christian Science church in search of some grounding. When I shared my location, the kind operator said, "Look across the street. See that dome? That's our church."

Suddenly I felt centered. And blessed.

Doubly blessed, actually, because the church was near the Royal Court, a famous theater. After spending the day as Nick Rivers singing "Skeet Surfing," a song about shooting skeet with a shotgun while surfing, I was ready for something serious. I walked the few blocks from my flat to experience what I hoped would be the glory of English acting. I don't remember much about the play, *The Genius*, but the lead actress, twenty-one-year-old Joanne Whalley, stole my heart. It wasn't the first time I had fallen in love, nor was it the first time I had fallen in love at first sight. But it was the first time I fell in love at first sight from a distance.

"The eye is the lamp of the body," said Jesus, "and if your vision is clear, your whole body will be full of light."

Looking at Joanne, I felt filled with light. The distance from my seat to the stage seemed the distance from earth to heaven. Joanne had a unique combination of beauty and toughness. (I later found out that she came of age in Manchester, a notoriously tough British town.) During the course of this play she wore a black leotard. Her body was perfect. Like a dancer, she was lighter than air. She floated. She possessed the dazzling grace of balance. The play was flawed, but she was

Joanne Whalley

not. I was overwhelmed. I desperately wanted to meet her. Yet I didn't. In explaining why, I may shock you.

I was shy. Yes, I was a performer. Yes, I was still dating Cher, although she was in California and I was in London. Yes, I was playing a swaggery rocker in a crazy comedy, but there nonetheless was an aspect of myself that in certain situations would retreat–retreat but also advance.

After each performance of *The Genius*, I waited by the stage door until Joanne emerged. I followed her and her fellow thespians down the street to the corner pub. I watched her drink, watched her smile, watched her exchange pleasantries with her peers, watched her laugh, watched her yawn, and watched her leave. I did not follow her further. I knew better than to stalk. I kept my distance and I never–not once– introduced myself.

What would I have said? *I'm Val Kilmer, starring as a rock star in a spy spoof. Surely, you've heard of* The Kentucky Fried Movie *and* Airplane! *Oh, you haven't. Well, let me explain. You see, it's a strangely American form of comedy . . .*

No. That wouldn't work. I didn't have a come-on line. I've never had come-on lines.

Despite my rebellion at THE Juilliard School, the place had made its mark. It had reinforced my notion of myself as a serious stage actor. And yet, here I was, floating in a sea of Hollywood fluff, however funny that fluff might have been. My rationalization was based on truth. It was based on Brando.

Brando is the benchmark. I read how he was crucified for taking the role of Sky Masterson in the film version of the musical *Guys and Dolls*, in which Frank Sinatra played Nathan Detroit. This was 1955, the year Brando had won the Academy Award for playing Terry Malloy in *On the Waterfront*, perhaps (along with Stanley Kowalski in *Streetcar*) his greatest role. I remember loving *Guys and Dolls* and loving Brando's performance. In one interview, when a reporter accosted him for selling out, he bristled and said he had done the film because it was the most challenging thing offered him. Even more so than playing Mark Antony in *Julius Caesar*. Why? Well, because he had to sing and he wasn't a singer. Not only did he sing, but he did so when his co-star was Frank Sinatra, America's most celebrated vocalist. That's the same kind of bravery that marked the careers of Katharine Hepburn and Charles Laughton, actors who traded in a euphoric emporium of art and dreams. They knew it's not about fame. It's about spirit. It was Brando who put in my head the idea that echoed my father's dream with the Native American: acting is about facing your fears and trusting that even if you fall off the cliff you are not going to die.

Actors who decry the entertaining aspect of acting miss the mark.

To act *is* to entertain. Brando was an outrageously enjoyable entertainer. Cher even more so. In my romantic life, I was Cher's boyfriend. That was a big deal.

To most of Hollywood, I was not yet a burgeoning talent but "Cher's lover." I have dog ears and could often hear industry folks whispering about us in fancy restaurants. Although not in Matsushia, where it was so loud with the joy in the room from the customers and waiters you could never hear any gossip even if it was happening at the table next to you. Cher had discovered this unknown establishment owned by Nobu Matuhisa, his first restaurant. He and I enjoyed each other from the beginning and are friends still. Perhaps that's why he still has movie posters up in the hallway to the bathrooms. That kind of Hollywood is almost all gone. It was fun while it lasted.

But back to Cher and gossip. Most of the time it was actually kind. *She's still got it.* But if you can believe it, we were less lovers and more best friends. Right from the start, it was all about curiosity and intellect. *What really is the aurora borealis? Have you been to see the Northern Lights? What about the Grand Canyon? You should go there.*

To star in a mainstream movie was nothing to sneeze at. Cher was mainstream. *Airplane!*, a hit comedy, was mainstream.

Meanwhile, my serious side got more serious. Back in my hotel room, I began writing poetry. I was rereading *Ulysses*, which Cher thought was somewhere between performative and ridiculous. The starting point had been "Sand," the verse that had helped me get into THE Juilliard School, which was followed by dozens of poems, some long, some short, some abstract, some narrative. My poems were necessary—even urgent—expressions of unformed ideas. I wasn't under the influence of any particular school of poetry. I liked Rimbaud, Yeats, Wallace Stevens. I liked Shakespeare's sonnets. But I wasn't a self-conscious writer.

Cher and I needed a moment. We would ebb and flow, separate and come back together, like two shiny fish. Enter . . . Michelle. I'd met Michelle Pfeiffer a few years earlier when we were both in an ABC Afterschool Special, *One Too Many*, about the dangers of teen drinking. Mare Winningham, also in the cast, got me the audition. I landed the role as a young alcoholic. Director Peter Horton and I spoke the same language. He was a Christian Scientist and also married to Michelle, who had an uncanny resemblance to Grace Kelly. Michelle and I became friends. She has a gentle, innocent soul. When her marriage to Peter hit a rocky patch, she confided in me.

Because he and I shared the same faith, I understood how Christian Scientists can display what seems like detachment when they're trying to commune with the Spirit. I had felt that distance in my own parents. I could talk to Michelle about that frustration—how I never felt the closeness to Mom and Dad that my heart desired. The secret pain

With Michelle Pfeiffer in the ABC Afterschool Special *One Too Many*

that Michelle and I shared created an intimacy between us. She had no one else to talk to about Peter; I had no one else to talk to about my parents. Plus, I had an all-consuming crush on Michelle's younger sister, who did not seem to reciprocate, even a little. In fact, she seemed to not even know I existed.

The minute *Top Secret!* wrapped, I felt I needed a break. My mind was swirling with affection for Cher, adoration for Michelle, and admiration for Joanne, the muse whom I'd never met. I needed fresh air. So I took all the per diem money I'd saved and backpacked through Europe. That silly little comedy had me half-crazy with excessive energy. I needed to unwind. I also saw that, as the star of the film, I had been getting spoiled rotten. When you have fifty people asking you ever so politely—remember, I'm in England for my first film at the world-famous Pinewood Studios where all the 007 films were made—when fifty people ask you all day long, "Is there anything you would like, Mr. Kilmer?" after a while, you start to answer them. When I woke up to this, I needed solitude. I needed to fend for myself. So I was off on my own, first to Scotland—Inverness, to be specific, the majestic city in the Highlands—then to Ireland, with an edition of Yeats in my back pocket, traipsing through the green countryside and reading out loud the poet's immortal "The Lake Isle of Innisfree."

I could see myself living alone forever, or at least for a few weeks. On the continent, I fell in love with Rodin. The photographs of his sculpture had not prepared me for the lyrical magnificence of the real thing. I discovered Calder. I loved the bustle of Europe but it wasn't until I set sail for the Maldives that I could really relax into the beauty of the sea. On the high waters of the Indian Ocean, I dreamed of meeting a young woman and set down my feelings in a poem I called "We've Just Met but Marry Me Please."

The Maldives are formed by coral curling into itself. The islands are tiny, convincing me that heaven must be tiny, a miniature world of flying fish of fantastical colorations, massive bundles of silver shimmering in the sunlight. I snorkeled until I was drunk with joy; my eyes ached from the beauty but my head ached for a seafaring Maldives experience that brought me to Malé, the main island. There I found the captain of a fishing vessel willing to take me to far-out ports. I explained how I had to be back in time for my flight to Africa, where I had booked a safari. Hemingway was much on my mind. The captain was cool but his crew wasn't. They were pirates whose thievery I narrowly escaped.

It was so surreal. I had never been on an island of pure natives, and most of the children had never seen a white man. As soon as we landed my crew vanished. After twenty-four hours I was more than nervous as I could not miss my flight, and it took much longer to get to the island than they told me. I couldn't find anyone who spoke English, and I realized the only way I could make any kind of statement and attract whatever authority was on the island was to deny their incredible hospitality. Virtually every hut I went to, trying to find my hiding crew, someone invited me to eat and enjoy what little they had. By refusing, this seemed to awaken in them the sense that I was somehow upset. On the morning of the third day, I was delirious and started to hallucinate from lack of food. I had a dreadful sense that I was in real trouble.

Perhaps I haven't mentioned it was against the law to go to an island that wasn't a "hotel island," which is exactly why I wanted this adventure. But this was more adventure than I had bargained for. I was in one of the huts, sweating and rocking in a hammock, when my first bit of hope arrived. It was a man who spoke English. I poured my story out in short bursts of dialogue, exhausted as I was by not eating. The kind man explained to me that there was no way off the island except for the crew that brought me. The reason he gave for them all disappearing was simply that they only came home once a year or so, and they were all off with their wives. Every one of these women with a beautiful daughter had been coming by my hut wanting me to marry them. I was also told by my new best friend that no one on the island could understand why I wasn't taking all these beautiful girls as my brides. "Brides?" I asked him. I didn't know much about their culture but I didn't recall polygamy as part of the program. He said no, it wasn't that–that all I had to do to get divorced was sort of clap my hands and wave them away and I was divorced. I explained I was rebelling against all manner of kindnesses like eating, until I met the chief or someone in authority who could help me. He said he could arrange a meeting with the chief and me.

"Great," I said, "the sooner the better," and at that moment I thought I heard a motorboat.

"No," my new friend said, "no engines here." The only way off the island other than the motorboat I came in was to go to the convict the authorities had put on this island to run the shortwave radio. He was taking a sailboat in a couple days, and if I had the money he could get me a passage on his sailboat to Malé, which would take three days.

"Impossible," I said emphatically.

Eventually the second of five daily prayer sessions rang out, and the friend said it was time to meet the chief. All the children followed me and rubbed my skin to see if it would come off. They laughed and laughed. It was impossible not to love them. All the English anyone knew was "Military? USA military?" My interpreter explained the war ships that passed through were all anyone knew of a white man. It was the first time I was made aware of the global power of our country. And how complete our reach was. Little children saw the white man and "military" was all they knew of us.

We arrived at the meeting hall, a simply constructed building with no partitions and a large roof that housed, I would guess, about a hundred people. It seemed the entire island showed up to watch the white man who refused to eat or get married.

My interpreter said, "The chief would like to know why you are here and what your problem is with your crew," pointing to my crew, which seemed to materialize before my very eyes. I told the chief my story, and then this Old Testament-style rhetoric just flew out my mouth.

"I want you to know, my kind host and these good people's king, that I will not ever use this crew or their boat, as they have been dishonest to me and might make me miss my airplane flight. I have no money to stay in the Maldives, but this is the truth, I will leave this island without their boat and its crew, and I challenge this young man"–I pointed at the smug young skipper of the boat–"I will pray to my God, and I ask him to pray to his, and if after praying to do what is right he still does not feel he has to give me back the money I gave him for this round trip and for gasoline I will not use, I will ask my God to deliver me from this island today."

Well, that sure got everyone's attention. The second my interpreter said "God" in his native tongue, the entire room fell silent. Then the afternoon prayer bell rang, right on cue. I've always had that sense of timing.

The chief spoke briefly to my former crew, after the interpreter finished, and pronounced our meeting finished. The children didn't follow me back to my hammock. The mothers did not bring their favorite beautiful daughters by. I fell in and out of consciousness and awoke out of a delirium thinking again that I heard an outboard motor, about half an hour before sunset.

The interpreter suddenly appeared out of breath and quite flustered. In my delirium I joked, "I could have sworn I heard a speedboat. Boy, I think I have to eat something."

"You can now, and you did," the interpreter said. "It's a miracle. There's a speedboat just docked on our landing."

I didn't waste a second, although I thanked my God for such a vivid answer to my prayer. Or edict. I have been told by spiritual practitioners it is sometimes all right to demand a sign.

After walking about a hundred yards, I kindly asked my friend to carry my backpack, as I just couldn't carry a full pack now, even heavier with beautiful seashells, remembrances from the Maldives, and whatever I had picked up in Europe. I came out of the village area with perhaps half the island occupants behind me. I have a clear memory that none but my friend would walk in front of me. It was either respect or fear or both that kept them all from making eye contact. And now comes one of these magical realism moments that I have myself made sure even in the moment to record in some forever part of my memory, knowing as I do that the brain plays tricks and it's easy to make believe or believe a dream as time moves on, but this is exactly what happened: The men and women who were singing on the beach, moving the catch of the day into baskets from the various nets from their fishing boats, all stopped singing as I came upon them, and parted as if in some well-rehearsed scene from a Cecil B. DeMille epic, and all in exact unison. Even as I remember remembering it I thought, "Never forget this happened exactly the way this is happening because in time you won't believe it." And then as the sun lit up the water and the sky simultaneously as it seems to do only in the most romantic seas and islands of the earth, the impossible revealed itself. Onto the cement dock where the good island people continued to part as if I were the alien I indeed now officially was, there floated before me with this impossible sunset behind it a massive double-decker speedboat, with two smiling Asian men discreetly but clearly wealthily dressed in casual sports clothes.

The one behind the wheel laughed and said loudly in perfect English, "You must be the American we have heard so much about!"

I snapped back as I took over my blue backpack, hoping to throw it on board without permission, "Yes, I am. And you must be the speedboat I thought I had dreamed of hearing a little while ago."

"Would you like a lift to Malé?"

"Yes, would you mind very much if I come aboard and hear your story on our way home?"

They agreed with much bright-eyed laughter and I bade my friend goodbye, never asking his name and never thinking I should let him hear the story of this miracle arrival as he was the one who spoke this prophecy to his island and his chief. It was a simple story. At the moment as I proclaimed to the chief that I would pray to my God, one of the Asian men, who owned a construction company that was contracted to build schools throughout the Maldives, got a call that his wife was headed to the hospital to have their baby. He hung up and suggested to his partner that instead of going to the closest school, they should go to the one farthest away for a final inspection. The man whose wife was going into labor could not say to his friend and partner why he wanted to go to the farthest one, especially because he had been anxious for days that he might miss the birth of his child unless he got on a flight right away. But now he was serene, he said to me.

"I told him, 'Everything will be fine and I will make it home to Japan in plenty of time.' "

I remember feeling warm, and I suppose the easiest way to say it is *out of body*. I just had a deep and abiding sense that I was in the presence of God, or Love, the love of Love. I felt a deep connection to this woman in Tokyo, and the baby inside her. And this man, and his partner who readily went along with his strange plan that would surely ruin his ability to make it to his wife on time.

Across the Indian Ocean we flew on this double-decker outboard motorboat of exceptional design. Perhaps my nameless friend had told them that I had not eaten in half a week, because before long a curry appeared before me. This simple meal is one of the great meals of my life. The great sushi chefs seem to relish the idea that they know just how to bend the minds of Westerners when they say, "Great sushi is always about the rice." But if you had eaten this curry and this rice that this ever-smiling man served me, the fluffy white rice that seemed to be made of warm snowflakes . . . I don't know how to describe the fluffiness of this rice. It was like eating cumulous clouds covered in chicken and curry sauce. I remember reminding myself to eat slowly. I remember that I did, before falling asleep, mid-chew, which is another thing I don't think I had done in days.

The wind, the sound of the twin motors, the laughter of the Japanese schoolhouse contractors, the joy of a full stomach: I could always know from this moment on that God is ever present, and the human picture just does not matter. That miracles are normal and to expect them. That this is not an arrogant act. It is, at times, a required act, demanding the presence of God. What an adventure.

I do not remember if I went to a hotel or straight to the airport. I remember that I had looked so many times at my airplane ticket that I thought I had actually gone mad, because I seemed to have refused to remember the date, or couldn't face the fact that I was going to miss my flight, and I had imagined all sorts of horrors. I had heard of jails

An early selfie at sea

and court hearings for American backpackers because of all the drug smuggling, and that they just assumed that's what you were doing if you weren't on a hotel island. I am so grateful for the answer to my prayer and wonder if I had obeyed the laws there, whether I could have had such a rare occurrence. I have to believe I could have, but I don't know how.

I scurried through the airport and made my flight. And then, after some ten hours in the air, for the first time I set foot on the continent that, more than any other, put me in touch with elemental forces that deepened my sense of the divine. Africa spoke to me in a voice as ancient as it was new. Nature assumed a grandeur I had not before experienced. I don't know how I had first fallen in love with Africa. I would like to say it was my whole life, as that's what it felt like, but it was likely sometime in high school. And then often in college I would fantasize about it with my brother Mark, how we would go on long safaris together once we were done with school. But we never did. When you dream dreams when you're young, do them before you have a reason not to. When you are young, that is when all the dreams come true. Believe me, do them all. Nothing bad will happen to you and all things good.

Africa was thrillingly complex and at the same time startlingly simple. It was basic. It was raw beauty. It was a polyphony of tribal and cultural currents I couldn't begin to comprehend. But I could observe. I could breathe in the air. I could gaze at the sky, watch the flight of exotic birds, hear the distant cries of animals, see the leopard, the tiger, the lion, the zebra, the gazelle, the giraffe, the noble elephant. Pay homage to all creatures. Thank God for this venture into territory that, once I arrived, would stay with me forever.

Sometimes when I go off on the crucial need to spend time with wildlife and sense I have lost my audience, often within seconds of my beginning, I circle back to the idea of shapes and sizes. I'll liken the creatures to cars or furniture or football players if that's what my listener is into, something that immediately engages the imagination, that seems to help explain why the simple experience of viewing fifty elephants in their train cross impossibly slowly across the savannah can change your life. They are magicians and force you somehow to look away, and suddenly when you look back at them they are miles and miles farther away from you. I know this is real because the giant dainty travelers have done this to me too many times to be coincidence. Perhaps it is their speech that's too low of a frequency for us to hear, that messes with human brainwaves. Perhaps some smarty-pants scientist has come up with the answer to this and I just haven't kept up on my African lore lately.

I still haven't taken my children. Practice what you preach, Val. Dream the big dreams and then do them.

Real Genius

F rom the unblemished wilds of Africa to the smog-covered San
Fernando Valley. Without quite realizing it, I was on a Holly-
wood fast track. My second starring role was in another comedy, *Real
Genius*.

I handled the whole audition arrogantly, and I'm afraid that arrogance might have won the day. The character was wildly arrogant,
with reason. He was the smartest person in the "smartest" school.

As soon as I arrived, the assistant to the assistant to the assistant
said, "Where's your headshot?"

"I don't believe in them," was my terse reply.

The assistant was so taken aback she didn't quite know what to do.
She whispered into the phone, and I went in to see director Martha
Coolidge (who'd recently had a hit with *Valley Girl*, a Romeo-and-Juliet
teen comedy with Nic Cage). Also in the room was a pre-spiky hairdo
Brian Grazer—a Hollywood mogul in the making. I did all this in the
character of the part I was looking to play—Chris Knight, a wise-guy
science whiz who finds a way to disrupt the CIA's demonic plan to

exploit his talent. I also brought four proper French croissants, and proceeded to devour one. The buttery crumbs dripped down my shirt, and everyone just stared at me like, *Is this guy for real?*

I'm not sure Martha or Brian knew what to do with me. I was standoffish but also committed. Very soon after we shook hands, Brian said he had to go and stood up. I stood up immediately, too, and said something like, "But didn't you say you were the . . . what was it? The . . . um, um . . . product man? What was it?"

"The producer," he said.

"That's right," I said. "That's what you said."

"Yes," he said, "but you stay and talk to Martha, she's the one you need to–"

"But you're the money guy! You're the one I want to spend time with. Wow! How DO YOU DO IT? Get people to fork over millions for this crap! You must be amazing! I will go where you go."

I babbled on following him out and down the elevator and tried to get into a cab with him, but that's when he finally drew the line. No crazy actor was going to get into his cab.

Somehow I was rewarded for all this silliness with the role. Also I remember demanding double the money I had any right to. I think that might have done the trick. I always think a forty-dollar hamburger *must* taste better than a Wendy's.

A cast member remembers something I don't: that after I'd been given the lead, I did the first read-through on my back, never giving eye contact to anyone, my focus completely on the script. It sounds like something a twenty-four-year-old young rocker like me would do. I have a vague memory of lying on the large plastic dining tables they fold out for events like this. Anything to establish the absolute weird-ness of the guy was fine by me, so I probably did do it.

Rehearsals were tricky. As one of the few female directors working in Hollywood at that time, Martha had my admiration, but she didn't see the humor the way I did. She identified with Chris Knight's headmaster—a villain/buffoon—and not with Chris himself. By giving the headmaster too much respectability, she undercut his laugh lines. I did my best to impose my comedic choices. This caused friction, so much so that one evening I came home from the set to a message on my answering machine from a colleague who said he'd just been asked to audition for the part of Chris Knight in *Real Genius*. In other words, *my* part.

I ran over to see Brian Grazer the next morning. He was bouncing a golf ball off his wall in a rhythmically hypnotic pattern.

"Hey, man," I said, "are you trying to fire me?"

Brian turned beet red.

"Martha says you're scaring the cast members," he responded. "You're not giving them a chance to be funny."

"The jokes aren't funny, Brian. And it's not funny when the headmaster is trying to be Hamlet. Come to rehearsal. Give me a little breathing room and I'll spread my funny around. You have some very talented comedians in the cast, but comedians always try to be funny. I get that, but it's not the comedy jokes the movie is about. It's about how all these smart kids don't know what my character is going to do next. That's what I'm establishing. Martha just doesn't get my humor. That doesn't mean it's not funny. Here, I'll prove it to you. Why is a Groucho Marx mustache funnier painted on than a real one?"

Brian is very smart, and I could tell it bothered him to have to answer what everyone *has* to answer.

"I don't know Val, why?" he said with the slightest bit of condescension. I really liked him and didn't like putting him on the spot like I had with Martha when I asked her the same question.

"I'm sorry, Brian, I'm not trying to give you a hard time. The

answer is, 'Who the hell knows why, it just is.' Comedy isn't intellec-
tual. You laugh or you don't. If you want, I'll stop making the film
better and get right down to the television laugh track it sounds like
everyone is into."

Brian relented. Martha relented. I was rehired before I was ever
fired. I got to do that fantastic scene when we're all swimming in a sea
of popcorn. It was delicious. It was also the perfect metaphor for a
popcorn movie. Martha let me make my own weird T-shirts, one of
which carried the exhortation "Surf Nicaragua." Decades later at
Comic-Cons I see fans wearing *Real Genius* custom-made T-shirts that
feature a gorilla I borrowed from the logo of my stepdad's secret men's
club.

Despite the fundamental disagreements between me and Martha,
the movie made good money. After we wrapped, cast member and
buddy of mine Jon Gries (who played Lazlo Hollyfeld, the brilliant re-
cluse who lives in a closet) and I drove across the country, curious to
see what the South was all about. Well, we learned that racism was
sure still an issue. We were actors determined to understand characters who were not part of our own background, so we hung out with
some serious rednecks. Those good ol' boys didn't play. They quickly
discerned where we stood on all the issues. Their next step would be
delivering upon us the punishment they knew we deserved. Before
that happened, we were well on our way to my new home in New
Mexico, our final destination, flying across the Mason-Dixon Line to
friendlier territory.

I had decided to make a documentary about nuclear power, and
New Mexico being the birthplace of the atom bomb I had no trouble
meeting people who not only had strong opinions about the nuclear
power subject but were actually part of its history. It is one of the more
bizarre parts of the history of this quiet little state that it also went

With actor Gabe Jarret in a publicity still for *Real Genius*.
The "International Order for Gorillas" T-shirt was modeled after
the logo of my stepdad's secret men's club.

through a period where its tranquility-inspiring scenery was the home of the most violent action we destructive humans have come up with in our short time of being the boss of this perfect ball of life we call Earth. Because of the madness capable in our flinty souls, we felt justified in coming up with a piece of equipment that not only would wipe out the enemy, it would also as a necessary part of its omnipotent destructive power take down everything else at the same time. This bomb blows up in both directions. It blows back as fast as it blows forward. But the fear was so extant—love that word—that we just figured to hell with the consequences. Gee, I wish we had thought that through a bit more.

To be sure, my documentary was a side trip, but side trips have been as important to my life as the main voyages. Maybe more important. I had read a ton of books about nuclear proliferation and was painfully aware of the government's cover-up. In fact, I was still going with Cher when she was making Mike Nichols's *Silkwood*, a cautionary tale, you'll remember, about a whistleblower (played by Meryl Streep) who works in a nuclear plant.

They were shooting in Texas and dear Cher brought me along for a number of dinners as she knew how much I loved Mike Nichols. I would soon outgrow him and directors who were early inspirations like Stanley Kubrick because I just found their enduring cynicism no longer part of what I needed art to do for me, and have since preferred a David Lean kind of classiness. But back then, I could hardly speak around Mike. He was one of the few people I was concerned about what they thought of me, especially because I was going out with someone like Cher, who is as vivid as a Fourth of July fireworks display in New Orleans on the centennial.

At those dinners, I was prepared to discuss the issue at hand and knew, when it came to information about the lethality of nuclear, I could hold my own. Nichols was a sparkling conversationalist but decided to make me the star of one particular evening by proving Stanislavski's axiom that the actor must be the most informed person in the room. So he asked me a lot of questions I wish I could have answered as well in a dramatic context in my little documentary. Cher was happy, and Mike was impressed. I didn't get much advice about how to finish my documentary, though.

Silkwood came out to great acclaim. Meryl, Cher, and Mike were all nominated for Oscars. The nuclear issue was galvanized. And I was dead set on making my own film about the crisis. It was called *Journey to Victory* because I wanted to assume optimism. I wanted to address both the hawks and the doves. Rather than alienate, I wanted to convince. Over a long period of time I interviewed everyone from five-year-old kids to eighty-five-year-old scientists. I shot in Washington, DC; New York; Germany; the USSR; and New Mexico. Whatever money I earned went into the film. But alas, the complexities of my life and career overwhelmed my determination to complete the project. I've had several such massive projects in my life, noble causes all. Sometimes they fly, sometimes they float, sometimes they sink. But no matter whether they are completed, they sustain me. I am not a practical man. I've never sought to be. It's not in my nature. Magical realism has an iffy relationship to practicality. It's not easily monetized. So my documentary on the dangers of nuclear is still unfinished. That doesn't make me happy. I'm still moved to open the can and complete the film. But if I don't do it now, it'll be for the same reason I didn't do it then: other projects emerge that, for one reason or another, cannot be delayed.

I do not know why the simple answer to my puzzle of how to make an entertaining film about the nuclear dilemma such as I understood it as a young man really required me to be in it. Somehow this thought never occurred to me back then—that it was my story of coming to an understanding about the most crucial issue of our time. At the time I just couldn't see what is now so obvious. The story is about me, not nuclear energy. But I just couldn't accept that I had to be on camera. I should have done one or the other, flown around the world learning from the people responsible for the nuclear dilemma or stayed in New Mexico and made a small film about our little state's strange central part in the development of all this violence.

The story is quite fascinating and weird. The heart of it is when our government realized that in order to build a bomb that could destroy all other bombs and life forms, they needed a secret place with plenty of room. Well, when Oppenheimer–the man the government put in charge of the project–was asked the question, he immediately suggested where he'd spent a few years in school where they send you away . . . I am blanking on what it's called . . . Hilarious. Anyway, when the Lindbergh baby was front-page news, wealthy families like the Oppenheimers chose to send their kids away where they would be safe from kidnappers. And New Mexico had such a summer camp-type school, just around the corner from where I ended up in Pecos, about a half hour east of Santa Fe, behind the gorgeous mountain range called Sangre de Cristo, the blood of Christ mountains, called so because of its hypnotically vibrant red clay that is beautiful and subtle all on its own, mixed in with the green of the majestic ponderosa pines and smaller pinyon pines that cover the landscape in rugged ragged display.

When the sun hits this red clay in the late afternoon the mountain just explodes into color that simply sings. Purple and blue and all ranges of red come in and out of powerful shades that make it sometimes impossible to drive around. More than once in the times I had the privilege to call New Mexico home, I would have to just pull over and take in the beauty, so overwhelmed as I was, just to be alive before the swirling colors and mixtures of nature demanding their place among the most beautiful settings on earth. They all have that mysterious final element which cannot be articulated, just what we end up calling magic. Something about the combination of elements in this place makes one giddy. A kind of childlike laughter wants to bubble up and flood out of you. Have you seen Will Ferrell's genius turn as a human raised by elves in Santa's North pole home where all the toys are made for Christmas? Well, that's the kind of happiness some of the images in New Mexico spark in me, and I think I can lay onto others. I have seen that picture welling up inside of Sam Shepard, although his macho quiet calm would never allow him to express himself so wildly in behavior, though perhaps in a theatrical setting and in the characters in his plays, often set in places very familiar to the New Mexican. A motel with no one in it. A bar with no one in it. A home with mainly a dark history as its sole occupant. You know, fun stuff you imagine is happening outside your window as you fly by on Route 66. Yes, there is a real Route 66. There was even a part of that old original highway on my ranch, which is now called Highway 25 in parts. But Route 66 is right there, right next to it, filled with Wild West history and connective tissue of the modern world which it seems will never rest until we've mowed it all down, the Great Plains soon little more than a series of golf courses, millions of golf courses. No matter how drought-ridden a place like New Mexico can be, let there be golf! What a poor substitute for real nature.

I have never understood the profound fear that forces us to trample every mystery in the wild until there is nothing left but that which is man-made, nothing to make our heart pump out of its chest. I am afraid it is not too far from now when we will wake up and it has all gone away. At least I got to raise my children on some little bit of its wild wild wind, some sunsets creating unspeakable magic onto the

Sangre de Cristos, the frozen warmth of the last run down to the Santa Fe ski lodge, the strange blue like a solid mist before the sudden snap of black that comes in winter when the sun has disappeared and hunger is about to completely envelop you until you hit Maria's and devour a combo platter as big as a spare tire. And then you wish you didn't have to be the driver, as you've no energy for anything but sleep or maybe to push the buttons on a remote and watch a Christmas comedy you've seen twenty times. But it isn't Christmas and a movie like *Elf* just isn't as special in July, so you let it fly and fall asleep dreaming of childhood gingerbread houses and drinks sprinkled with cinnamon and other old country treats you just can't duplicate from store-bought stuff, even as good as Whole Foods has managed to produce.

Father & Son

A strange thing happened on my way to stardom, no matter how minor that stardom might have been. My father, Eugene Kilmer, reentered the picture. The truth is that my father never left the picture. In trading Chatsworth for THE Juilliard School, I made my great escape. Although I came back to LA to be with Cher and make movies, I kept a place in New York. I needed distance between me and Dad, and I have always loved the City that Never Sleeps for all its swirling greasy grandeur. I thought I had escaped my father, but I hadn't. Geographical distance is one thing. Emotional distance is another. I think of Screamin' Jay Hawkins's classic "I Put a Spell on You." Maybe all fathers put spells on all sons. They are and will always remain Our First Man. And I suppose, being well aware of the Oedipal myth that demands a son must powerfully negate his father to become his own man, I felt the negation was fully realized. I was my own man, an actor, an independent spirit.

But I wasn't my own man. I was Eugene's son, and as such, when he called I responded. He called at an especially critical time in his life.

His fantasies of becoming one of California's prime landowners had not been realized. He had made foolish moves—I suspect the loss of his youngest son was responsible—and his finances were eroding. He needed loans. And to secure those loans he asked me, who was finally landing roles that paid well, to cosign his notes and deals. I did so. I nearly wrote, "I did so willingly," but I'm not at all sure how willing I really was. I was under that inexplicable fatherly spell. Why not help the old man? Besides, for all his bluster, I had inherited his energy and ambition. I'm not sure I thought twice about it. Documents were put before me. I was given a pen. I signed. Before I knew it those notes and deals had gone down the toilet, Dad had millions of dollars in liabilities, and I was on the hook for all of it. It took a decade to pay it off. My father and I were proud men. We never wanted to burn our creditors. That pride led us both into financial turmoil. Was it his fault? Or was it my fault? A little of both.

Either way, the Oedipal drama turned epic. For the most part, the drama was silent. We didn't say much to each other. When I had my voice, I couldn't bring myself to tell my father what was in my heart. Now that I don't have my voice, I am ready to say what remained unsaid. I was resentful. I was dutiful. I was cowed. I wanted to say, "Dad, these are your problems. You solve them."

So I took on the debt, and wrote a check for $1.2 million, an act that proved my inability to disengage myself from my father's unrelenting drive. In the material world, my primary drive is artistic. It isn't that I don't like or want money. I like it just fine and I want it. I love buying stuff. I love giving away stuff. But I didn't become an actor and writer with the idea of making a fortune. I did it because it was my nature to do so. I never even made the choice. And though I did make the choice to cosign Dad's deals, I really didn't anticipate the burden. On the simplest level, I was just trying to be a good son. But being a good son, at least with a father as complicated as Eugene Kilmer, would never be simple. His declining years as a speculator coincided with my ascending years as an artist. More and more, he was his own version of King Lear on the heath, riddled with shame, guilt, and confusion. Since Wesley's death, his sense of self had eroded. That made me sad. He was a mountain of a man, but no longer.

New Mexico Is Called the "Land of Enchantment" or, as I'm Proud to Have Coined, the "Land of Entrapment"

G row it as it goes." That's the slogan for New Mexico, taken from an ancient poem by the Roman philosopher Lucretius. It's an apt description of my relationship to a state that plays a huge part in my story, where people aren't the only characters. Places can be major characters. In introducing the character of New Mexico, my original intention was to write a long list of everything that is wrong with the state. *It's so touristy. All strip malls. Be careful of the fake turquoise.* The idea was to scare people away so New Mexico would not suffer from overcrowding and all the other deadly drawbacks that come with un-checked invasion. I wanted to echo Georgia O'Keeffe, who said, "When I got to New Mexico . . . I saw it . . . was my country . . . It's something that's in the air—it's different. The sky is different . . . I shouldn't say too much about it because other people may be interested and I don't want them interested." (O'Keeffe also said, "I hate flowers—I paint them because they're cheaper than models and they don't move.")

But although I feel protective about my adopted state, I cannot restrain myself. I must extol its glorious virtues. Go there, relish its beauty, but please clean up after yourselves and leave ever-so-light carbon footprints. Thank you.

It's a cliché, or perhaps critical to my sensibility, that after my childhood visits with my family I rediscovered New Mexico through a siren of sorts, a fascinating woman with a boring name: Jane Smith. We met at Hollywood mega-agent Sue Mengers's house. I was brushing shoulders with superstars . . . when Michael Jackson walked in. He had a lady on his arm who was one of the most gorgeous people I'd ever witnessed, whom he discarded like an umbrella as soon as he walked in the door. As he moved through the room, heads turned like we were in a choreographed commercial, and he was beelining for none other than my own former girlfriend, Cher.

I was in my twenties, Jane in her forties. By then Cher and I were no longer a couple. If I could describe our breakup, I would. But I can't because it never really happened, at least not formally. She never said, "Val, I'm through with you," and I never said, "That's it, Cher. We're history." Our histories ran on parallel tracks. Our friendship deepened. We just moved on.

Jane Smith had a wealthy swagger about her. She spoke about her home state, New Mexico, as though she were speaking of a long-lost soul mate. When she invited me to visit her there, I did. She was living with a locally famous lesbian, Betty Stewart, who was not Jane's lover but a strong partner. They cherished each other. Betty was famous for building classic territorial-style triple-thick adobe homes for millionaires across Santa Fe. She was part artist, part builder. Everyone warned me as soon as they found out I was staying in one of Jane's guest rooms on Betty's property that I was likely to wake up with a gun in my face or something similarly dramatic, but to their surprise Betty and I got along immediately and famously. I don't know why or how. Perhaps it's that she hailed from Texas and my father was born in the panhandle. Texans like that about me, and I don't mind sharing that fact within the first two minutes of meeting a Texan. The saying is true: don't mess with them about their state, or they will spend the rest of the night telling you about how they have seriously contemplated seceding themselves from our great experiment.

But back to New Mexico, a state in which you are obligated to treat people right. Years later, as New Mexico became my spiritual home, I befriended Sam Shepard, who exemplified those deeply human qualities of empathy and compassion. So while it was a mortal goddess who initially called me back to my ancestors' land, I believe it was the God of Love that had me return again and again to the state, where, like my father, I longed not only to live on its land but to possess a large parcel of it for myself. That parcel was precious. I loved it and lost it. But all that's later. And my heart still aches.

In my early trips to New Mexico I had, in addition to my connection with she of the wealthy swagger, another pivotal experience. This one was seismic. I encountered an angel. I was wide awake. I was indoors. It happened on my birthday. I had just turned twenty-four. I was asleep and awoke suddenly to an amorphous black figure before me. It will ruin the absolute gravity of this moment but in truth this dark angel looked very like Darth Vader, though without the helmet. The figure seemed to be covered in a black shroud that every now and again revealed the slightest outline of a face. It took up space in an infinitely eternal way. I was afraid.

I addressed it by saying in my mind, "I can feel you reading my mind."

He replied, "That's not what's happening."

Well, that proved it, didn't it? It's indescribable when someone or thing can read your mind, and I said so—or thought it.

"I have nowhere to hide."

I knew this was a sacred encounter and yet, like Mary or Moses, I felt fear. He then reached in, extracted my heart, and held it before me. It had a purple-blackish hue, leading me to joke, "Is it that bad?"

"No," he said. "I'm just giving you a bigger one."

The bigger heart, spinning rather than beating, was placed inside my body.

At first I thought it was the Angel of Death before realizing it was the Angel of Life. I wish I could elucidate the experience more than I have already done, but I can't. It simply happened. I remember pinching myself as hard as I could in hopes of bruising myself, so that if I fell back asleep or was put to sleep by this dark angel, I would be able to prove to myself this was a real experience. I looked at my clock and noticed it was moments before I was born that morning twenty-four years ago. Somehow the spell was over, and just as I thought, I did fall fast asleep and woke up the next day with a bruise on my arm. I have nothing else to say about this, except that I am grateful for the new heart. It has served me well. And I've only just begun to use it.

I have always affirmed life in the spiritual realm. At the same time, I love living and the beauty of shapes and the variety of life in the material world. That Love is undergirded by the rigors of backpacking. I am a backpacking freak. I devoured books like Colin Fletcher's *The Man Who Walked Through Time*, his riveting chronicle of trekking from one end of the Grand Canyon to another. So when I got word that Hollywood genius Jeffrey Katzenberg was organizing a rafting trip down that same canyon, I was waiting for an invitation that never came. It's the only time in my career I was jealous of Tom Cruise—and this was before *Top Gun*. Jeffrey included Tom on the list. Was that because his star turn in *Risky Business* outshined my turn in *Top Secret!*? Or was it Tom's publicist? Well, if it was the publicist, I'd hire her. Except she wasn't buying me. She suggested I employ a less powerful flack who specialized in selling pretty faces. Forced humility is always good for the soul, but I can't say I was happy. I decided to go with no publicist at all.

Then came a blissful surprise of a romance. I encountered Ellen Barkin, who had the best smile in all five boroughs. She was a proud native of the Bronx. Our romance was as whimsical as it was whirlwind. This was after she'd been in *Diner* with Mickey Rourke and *Tender Mercies* with Robert Duvall. I remember her wit, her sultry eyes, but mostly her laugh. And her hair. Who remembers the softness of a woman's hair? If you ever have a chance to consensually ever-so-gently touch Ellen's hair, it will be worth the look she's gonna drop on you. Ellen has a helluva stare. I was crazy for her, and we had some fabulous months window-shopping on Rodeo Drive by day and barbecuing at night, crushing ice and swishing lemons and limes in one of those weird board games of summer love. Ellen was one of the enchantresses who got away, no doubt due to my unmanageable preoccupations, my neglect. I want to call it benevolent neglect, but I'm afraid that term is a bit too self-serving. Is it enough to say that when it comes to women, I'm a fool? In my defense, I want to cite a thousand popular songs. I want to avoid the entire subject of my relationship to women. But I can't, and I won't. All I can do is try my damndest to be honest—honest about my absolute failings to take advantage of the scores of opportunities afforded me by the answer to prayers. As I wrote in my one-man show *Citizen Twain*, about the honorary founding father: "I think it ain't that prayer doesn't work, it's that we don't like the answers."

Romance among actors is no simple matter. We are always on edge and always on the move. The phone rings and we're off to London or back to LA from New York. We're not only driven to perform our craft but also propelled, like athletes, by the inbred competition of show business. We run into each other at parties, on backlots, in agents' offices. We kiss, we hug, we wish one another well. We mean it, we don't mean it, we feel bad for not meaning it. But our drive—whose source remains a mystery—does not diminish. Therefore romance is at once a necessity, a delight, and its own special thrill.

As I've said concerning artistic projects, I am subject to distraction. I am subject to impetuosity. The same goes for romance. I take it seriously. I accept these liaisons as lovely interludes. Some lasted for years, some for months. All last forever.

I Did *Top Gun*, Son

I didn't want the part. I didn't care about the film. The story didn't interest me. My agent, who also represented Tom Cruise, basically tortured me into at least meeting Tony Scott, saying he was one of the hottest directors in town and I could never afford to not meet with as many of them as possible, and also he was completely obsessed with me. Well, an agent doesn't have to offer any other reasons when "the director is completely obsessed with you" comes out of their mouth.

I showed up at the audition because that's what actors do when they're asked to audition. I showed up looking the fool, or the goon. I wore oversize gonky Australian shorts in nausea green. I read the lines indifferently. And yet, amazingly, I was told I had the part. I felt more deflated than inflated. I had to get out of there.

The moment I got into the elevator, the director ran after me and slid his arm in to block the door. He blurted his truth in his chipper British accent: "I know that the script is insufficient, but it will get better, Val. Wait until you see these jets. They take your breath away." He then proceeded to imitate aircraft sounds and motions as if we were six years old and as if there were no one else in the hallway. "I know you've been told this before, I know you're a serious actor, but you are perfect for this role. It's as if they wrote it for you. It has to be you. It's not the lead, but I'm going to make you feel like it is. And this kid we found, Tom Cruise, he has it, man, and you two together, and Kelly McGillis—you know her from Juilliard, she's nine feet tall and utter perfection."

He was a wrecking ball to my consciousness. I had never before been treated with such passion. I was so accustomed to giving passion, less familiar with receiving it.

Side note: I once flew to London when I couldn't afford a ham sandwich to sit in a hotel room with a single videotape in hopes of hand-delivering it to Stanley Kubrick. Eventually I befriended one of his "people," who told me after my forty-eighth phone call in one week, "I'm sorry, Val. He really liked the last video you did. I am not supposed to say this, but he's really interested. In fact, we have stopped pre-production because of that last video. But he won't see you. He just doesn't work like that."

Self-taping was new at the time, and Kubrick must have been enchanted with it. I got it. I was enchanted myself and had been shooting me and my friends since I could get my hands on a magical machine of my own. But Kubrick's stubbornness sent me home, deflated.

Tony Scott's British enthusiasm was the pick-me-up my ego craved. He was ferocious and hilarious. We both had penchants for fishermen's vests. His was primly packed with pens, folded paper, and cigars, plus a monocle cinematographers use to examine the sun. Now video cameras adjust to let you film through the night, but it wasn't like that back then.

Tony loved the process, loved the energy of the set, loved the characters. Everything was fuel to Tony. Every time a jet took off, Tony swooned. I threw lines away. He would jump for joy. Ultimately, he overwhelmed my disdain for the project with pure un-adulterated positivity. Every day he would exclaim, "This is incredible! This is beautiful! This is beyond belief. You guys are going to be kings."

Off set, the actors broke into two camps—mine and Tom's, a reflection of the rivalry between our two char-

Tony Scott

acters. In the film, I was Iceman and Tom was Maverick. I commanded my camp because I had a tricked-out van.

We were the party boys. Every night we'd hit the San Diego nightlife. Once we were stuck at an intersection where all four lights were red. I peeled out, spinning and burning rubber in a perfect circle, showing off. Until we cozied right up to a cop car. He looked at me like, *Really, dude?*

He didn't even bother turning on his lights. I just pulled over and begged my drunken passengers, in my firm Iceman voice, to sit up straight and to let me do all the talking. Since I hadn't been drinking, I was able to quickly rely on my actor's instinct.

"Where's the fire, boys? License and registration." I snapped my fingers as if Rick Rossovich, who played the pilot Slider, worked for me. He popped open the glove box, and I started. "Officer, the fire is in my producer's eyes. It's entirely my fault but we're about forty minutes late for the movie we are shooting down here called *Top Gun*."

"Oh, *Top Gun*. Yeah, I've heard of it. My brother is a pilot."

"Oh, a real pilot. Outstanding. We're a bit lost. Perhaps you can point us in the right direction."

"It smells like a frat party in here."

"Yes, officer. I'll tell these bozo ruffians to shower."

"All right, then. Go on. Be careful. And take it easy. That was some crazy driving, son."

"Yes, sir. And best to your brother, sir."

The uncannily blessed lives that actors lead. A privilege of uncountable latitude.

Tom refrained from our revelry, with good reason. From day one, he was laser-focused on a singular goal: to become the greatest action hero in the history of film. He was up nights learning lines; he spent every waking hour perfecting his stunts. His dedication was admirable. Of course even more admirable is the fact that he achieved his goal. I also love that he's a Mark Twain fan. Tom is a comrade I respect and admire, though as creatures we hail from galaxies far, far away from one another.

My favorite moment between us was a small prank in which I gave him an extremely expensive bottle of champagne but placed it in the middle of a giant field and made him follow scavenger-hunt-style clues to find it. I hid behind a bleacher and watched him lug the giant crate to his motorcycle. He never did thank me for the Iceman-style bit. I thought it would break the ice, but I guess the ice was just right.

All in all, the movie was both a blast and an education. I hear the voice of poet Ezra Pound, who, in one of his cantos, wrote, "Pull down thy vanity," but I am afraid my vanity is about to be put on full display. Take the famous volleyball game. It was a real game with all us showing off our pecs. Because I was the only Californian in the match, I was

As Tom "Iceman" Kazansky

actually the only real volleyball player and couldn't help but demonstrate my best moves. We got loads of sweaty, sexy close-ups. I was happy with the day's work until Tony ran up to me the next day looking like he'd seen a ghost.

"Horror of horrors," he said. "We overexposed some of the film and your close-ups have been ruined."

I wasn't happy and wouldn't have minded a reshoot of the entire scene, but that was not within my purview. Tony was genuinely remorseful and I let him know that, as proud as I was of my physique, a little less cheesecake would hardly hurt the film. Besides, certain moments that I had improvised, like spinning the ball on my finger and the trash-talking locker room scene, made it into the film. I must also take partial credit for the weird crew cut I sported. The style was Tony's idea, but I went out of my way to make it weirder. When it turned into a national fad—thousands of guys started emulating the coif—I was flabbergasted. And that's a word you just don't get to say that often and mean it.

Another point of pride was flying in the jets. Though I was never really doing it, I learned the mechanics of operating the plane. We all went up in the jets several times and—here comes more vanity—I have to report that I was the only one who didn't regurgitate, which, given the gut-wrenching drops and spins of those ferocious flights, was no mean feat.

The servicemen loved partying with us. At one such fête, a flyboy came up and said, "Val, you're the one who operates like a real pilot." With each word of praise, he struck my chest—all in the spirit of manly goodwill—until he left a silver-dollar-size bruise that took weeks to heal.

And then, just like that, our real-world counterparts, our advisers, were gone. They had to fly off on a secret mission. At the outset, I saw *Top Gun* as jingoistic, but in the spring of 1986, about a month before the release, the US carried out airstrikes on Libya for terrorist attacks at airports in Vienna and Rome, which gave the film a relevance it had previously lacked.

As filming went on, I grew more serious about my on-screen character. Even though I could play an arrogant jerk in my sleep, I actually found myself looking deeply into this guy. What made him arrogant? The question intrigued me. I thought about it for long stretches of time. Even dreamed about it. And then, without any forethought, I applied whatever I had learned (or unlearned) at THE Juilliard School, whatever I had read of Stanislavski and Suzuki, whatever natural instincts I had, and brought it all to bear in Tom "Iceman" Kazansky. I became so obsessed that at one point in my trailer I actually saw—the way Macbeth saw the ghost of Banquo—Iceman's father, the man (my imagination told me) who had ignored his son to the point where his son was driven to prove himself as the absolute ideal man. So real was the elder Mr. Kazansky that I saw him take a chunk of ice and chew on it like a wild dog (which inspired my improvised ice-chewing and teeth-chomping moment in the film). I even spoke to him. As Iceman, I asked him, "What do you want of me, Dad?"

He answered, "To stay on your journey."

"What journey is that?" I asked.

"A journey," he said, "for the clergy. You're on a journey for the clergy."

I'm not sure I understood that exchange, but I am sure that this encounter with Iceman's father imbued my character with greater fury.

The only person who honored the process more than me, I think, was our brilliant Tony. One day at dusk, we were up in a helicopter. He was trying to get a perfect angle on the aircraft carrier where most of the film takes place, and I was along for the ride.

I couldn't understand what he was trying to capture. There were so many fumes and we were losing the light, and I thought he might be going mad. And then, suddenly, the clouds were rainbow sherbet, and you could see circles of rainbow smoke curling, falling on the water as the aircraft carrier danced its dance. Just like Tony had dreamed. It was incredible. I glanced over to smile at him or give him a little nod, and as I turned toward him, tears were rolling down his cheeks.

When I finally saw the film for the first time, on the Paramount lot, I jumped up after the first five minutes and yelled, "This is a hit!" The editing and sound were stupendous. The minute it was over I made a mad dash across the lot to the office of the film's producers, Don Simpson and Jerry Bruckheimer, past their assistants, and into the royal quarters, where the prince himself, Simpson, was seated behind his massive desk.

"Don," I screamed with stars in my eyes, "you've done it!"

Jerry looked up at us both. Don's response to my declaration was to jump on top of his desk, clad in his signature cowboy boots, and assume the pose of a cartoon superhero. His stance was earned, and I cheered. It was so wild a move from Don as to be normal.

In the final analysis, *Top Gun*'s iconic endurance is the result of the untiring dedication of Don, Jerry, Tony, and Tom. Optimism can work wonders. Infusing things with light was a sport Tony Scott had mastered, and one I would emulate for many years to follow.

Ah, Tony, Tony, Tony. I don't know why you killed yourself, but I miss you almost every damn day. In 2012, Tony drove to the Vincent Thomas Bridge in San Pedro, and jumped off the highest point.

When Tony was making a television show that needed a bit of a face-lift, he asked me to appear. Despite the fact that I hated TV, I didn't hesitate. I'd hang around him as we filmed and just observe. Tony and I would wake up and have coffee on a bridge near our set every morning at dawn, overlooking the Mississippi River. So when he jumped, I almost felt like I had a memory of it.

You're So Twain (Carly)

I'd been to a concert of the divine Who. The Who had done it. Right in our faces. It was a starlit night when the wonderful voodoo Who smashed through time. With their heady mix of vanity and humble homage to the rock gods that birthed them, the Who had blasted our brains for hours on end. No chance of sleep. Parties and camaraderie till the wee small hours in the Big Apple. Now it was time to head home.

The city streets were empty. In my mind, I heard Paul Simon singing "The Only Living Boy in New York." Moments later, I imagined my old friend Peter Gabriel crash-landing and floating over my head like a million monarch butterflies, crooning tunes from *The Lamb Lies Down on Broadway*. It was an oddly soft daybreak, when the island is usually overrun with traffic and people and police and maids walking their owners' dogs. This morning, though, was different. New York had found a temporary lull, and I, walking its concrete canyons, was in the center of the calm. The only sound was the *ca-clack ca-clack* of my genuine Beatle boots, which I'd bought on St. Mark's Place, boots

I'd been wearing so long that I'd walked off the life of the rubber but didn't care. Those boots could never leave my feet. They directed me to where I needed to go, and this morning I needed to go on this stroll for reasons I could not fathom until I quickly approached an intersection where, standing on the corner, waiting to cross the street, was a woman who looked like Carly Simon. It was Carly Simon. Carly Simon was facing me. She on one side of the street, I on the other, waiting for the green light to turn red.

The *ca-clack ca-clack* of my Beatle boots and the *ca-clack ca-clack* of my heart beat in the same frantic rhythm. The rhythm was too frantic. I had to slow down. I didn't want to; I wanted to run across the street, fall on my hands and knees, and testify to my love of her music and her smile and the sheer see-through summer dress that revealed more than my eyes could absorb. I wanted to scream, wanted to declare my devotion to a woman I had never met. I wanted to do handstands and somersaults while declaiming Shakespearean soliloquies and quoting the sexiest passages from the Song of Songs. I wanted to tell her how I had discovered the secrets of her music from *No Secrets* and knew all the pain that she, a shy woman, had endured because shyness had also been my lifelong companion, which was a secret I was willing to reveal only to her. I wanted to tell her everything but shyness kept me from saying a word. And then the light changed and we were approaching one another. Humming "Anticipation," I told myself that if she smiled or even waved at me, then yes, we would meet again.

She walked off the curb. I walked off the curb. And she did smile, a smile radiant enough to wash over me like a sacred salve, and she walked right by me with all the poise of a fairy-book princess.

If our first encounter was encased in eerie solitude, our second unfolded in hysterical mayhem. It was the massive after-party for the opening of *Top Gun*. For some reason, the premiere was in New York.

Celebrities were flitting about like fireflies, champagne flowing, strobe lights flashing, paparazzi straining to break through the VIP velvet rope guarded by an army of real fighter pilots, or so it seemed. I had arrived with Cher. Our romance was ancient history but our friendship forever fresh. Cher, though, had wandered off and I couldn't find her. That was unusual. Not being able to find Cher is like being in the Sahara and not being able to find the sun.

But no matter. We were good friends, and I wasn't jealous. Cher had many men. Every time David Geffen, one of her main men, sees me, he points and declares, "When it comes to Cher, there's only one man I've ever been jealous of. Oh, that Cher . . ." He makes a fist and shakes it at the air before adding, "She said she loved you best, but what do you got that I ain't got? Don't answer that."

And then, there was Carly, dressed simply, dressed elegantly, standing next to a woman and appearing accessible. My courage was up. We were not standing on a street corner. We had both just seen a film in which I was one of the top guns. I could approach. I could walk right up to her and say, "If I gave you my number, would you call me?"

"Yes."

"Do you remember we sort of met once?"

"I would have remembered."

She had a way of making me feel completely stupid and not mind it. I usually don't like feeling stupid at all. Ever. But I was happy as hell; like the Iceman village idiot, I might've even giggled. (I am sweating, nervous about-to-go-onstage palm sweat, as I write this.)

She called a week later and invited me to her apartment, only about ten blocks from mine. Carly's home on the Upper West Side looked and felt and smelled exactly like you would dream it. We talked all day about everything under the sun. We talked about shyness. We talked about Harry Nilsson. We talked about Bob Dylan and Dylan

Thomas and the evils of yellow journalism and the exquisite phrasing of Frank Sinatra. We talked and talked and talked. We had dinner. The hour grew late and then Carly asked, "Would you like to stay in my guest room?"

I would. She bade me good night. I slept alone, slept like a baby, dreaming dreams in which I made the music of the spheres. In the morning she greeted me with a tray of perfect organic eggs and jams from her favorite shop on Martha's Vineyard, where she'd been going since forever. It was the best breakfast of all time. I wanted to be with Carly every day of the rest of my life.

"I wrote a song yesterday for Mike Nichols's next film," she said. "Would you mind listening to it?"

I would not mind. I probably would have jumped right out the window overlooking the unspeakably beautiful Central Park if she'd even mildly hinted that it might make her happy. She had utter power over me. As she played her acoustic guitar and sang with a sultry subtlety that is Carly's and Carly's alone, I have no idea how I kept from kissing her, but I did.

Our friendship flowered. She invited me back to her apartment, where her grand piano overlooked Central Park, and she played original songs she considered too anemic to record. I considered them soulful masterpieces. She often spoke of her children, Ben and Sally. I think the reason we soon stopped seeing each other was her realization that it was too overwhelming for me. Her shy sensitivity saw through my soul.

She saw that I was madly, hopelessly in love with her. I'm not sure I ever spoke those words, but you must have known, Carly. You, being so wonderfully well-read; you, being so openhearted; you, having grown so gracefully from your auspicious family tree; you, having blossomed into an artist of singular enduring beauty. There is surely a hidden and seamless sweetness to your craft, Carly, and to your very nature. And it is not the sweetness of sugar, no. It is a more wholesome, salty sweetness, the sweetness of honey. The beauty of the bees, the way that they alchemize nature, that's what you do in your music. And all I can do is thank the holy spirits that, despite a shyness that is as endearing as it is painful, you have expanded the sky.

Let's Go Upstairs

S uddenly I felt I had to leave New York. I no longer wanted to wake up in the city that doesn't sleep. In fact, I no longer *could* wake up. Because I was never going down. The literal and spiritual electricity is crazy. If you want authentic Maldivian fish at three in the morning, you can find a cool place or even have it delivered. Beyond everything I loved—the art and theater and music and dance—beyond its beating avant-garde heart and its pulsating creativity, its dirty bricks were almost burned with the energy, and they weighed heavily on my soul. I wanted to feel open and wild and free. To be in a place defined by spirit, not responsibility.

L.A. was not a possibility. Growing up there, it held no exoticism whatsoever in my mind. I remember recently I ran into a close friend and fellow native Angeleno, Angelina Jolie. We were on an airplane heading back to LAX, and her children were sprawled across many seats, sleeping peacefully. She whispered, "All I ever wanted to do was leave this city, and now look at me." As rooted as roots can be.

No, a home in the Hollywood Hills or a spread in Brentwood or

Beverly Hills held no interest for me. I confess to harboring hatred for the San Fernando Valley, scene of my childhood. I consider it the bottom rung of hell. In saying that, though, I must acknowledge the gifted director Paul Thomas Anderson, who in *Boogie Nights* and *Magnolia* was able to show me the improbable and (up until his films) invisible beauty of the Valley. It was also Paul who introduced to me the genius of Philip Seymour Hoffman. He didn't star in *Boogie Nights* or *Magnolia*, but he illuminated both films. I was wild for his work. I watched his every movie and marveled at his craft. There are scores of superb actors but some, like Philip, have a mystical ability for complete transformation. I think of Gene Hackman, Daniel Day-Lewis, Meryl Streep, Hilary Swank, and Peter Sellers, to name a few. Philip ranks in the highest of dramatic categories.

I lacked Paul Thomas Anderson's fresh eyes in viewing the expansive Los Angeles landscape and instead fled to Santa Fe. Ever since being drawn there by my father throughout early childhood, I had liked everything about the town, especially the vibrant community of sculptors, painters, and poets. I found a fabulously funky house, half of which was for rent. Its owners were several brothers who lived with their mother, stricken by a stroke and confined to a wheelchair but once infamous in Santa Fe for throwing parties that attracted the bohemian community. I had heard that once the merriment got under way and the music was blaring, Mom would lift her dress to reveal panties whose lettering read, "Let's Go Upstairs."

Despite my fear of someone spiking my morning coffee with acid, it seemed like the house where I wanted to live. It was funky and offbeat, with a screw loose, like everything great in what was left of the Wild West.

The sole moment of hesitation came when I was about to sign the lease and the Realtor, respecting his obligation for full disclosure, mentioned that one of the brothers had been convicted of murder. Pause for thought. I decided to confront the siblings. "I've heard that one of your brothers is in prison for murder," I said matter-of-factly.

"Well, yeah, our older brother, but he's out now, and he feels real bad about it."

I signed the lease.

Those years were marked by the presence of a woman in my life whom I never expected to meet again. She was the same woman who had been running through my dreams since the first time I saw her. I didn't try to meet her. It happened, though I don't know how. Saying I am lucky is an insult to belief and to the will of God. I surrendered to that will, but I suppose I was not above tampering with the timing. I wanted this woman and was in a great hurry to win her love.

WE'VE JUST MET BUT MARRY ME PLEASE

Hello, let's find out about forever together and
Will you purchase Sen-Sen?
Will you be my gal?
Will you shine that big roller coaster up into the sky?
Will you give me grown-up feelings?
Will you kiss my eyes?
Will you buy me flowers?
Will you send one by? And
Will you bury me?

Bury me?
Bury me?
Bury me?
Bury me when I die?

—Indian Ocean at sea, 1982

Willow

I had turned down David Lynch's *Blue Velvet* and *Dirty Dancing*. I had done so with little regret. Neither part spoke to me. In the aftermath of their success, though, regret did rear its ugly head—I am not, after all, immune to "could have"s or "should have"s. We all have misgivings, yes we do. I wish I had not said no to so many brilliant directors. Like Robert Altman. I loved his films and really respected his willingness to follow his heart and just make smaller films when Hollywood seemed to feel the need to punish him for his expensive misfire with *Popeye*. We all make mistakes. But have you seen *Nashville* lately? And David Lynch I turned down more than once. I had loved him since seeing his first film, *Eraserhead,* but the original script for *Blue Velvet* was, in my opinion, a high-quality porn film. It seemed to me that David was aspiring to make a XXX-rated film. It had extremely graphic depictions of sex acts, and I was just too much of a conservative spirit about sex to participate in celebrating it in that way. There was just no way. I sure wish he would have called me when he changed his mind about how to best dramatize his extremely compelling ideas.

Maybe it's not too late. Maybe one day we can finally work together. A character who lives up on Mulholland and doesn't speak much? David, I am so sorry I never explained myself.

Instead, I signed onto *Willow*, a massive George Lucas production directed by Ron Howard that was expected to become *the* blockbuster of 1988. I was cast as Madmartigan, a swashbuckling, overenergized swordsman. The real hero, though, is Willow himself, masterfully played by Warwick Davis, whose journey to realize his potential as a sorcerer sets the story in motion.

I flew to London and visited the production office to see who would be cast as my costar, the gorgeous warrior Sorsha, who, by falling in love with me, betrays her evil mother. Even now as I see the aspiring actress walk into the room to read the lines, my heart beats as loudly as it beat three decades ago. It was Joanne Whalley, the woman whom I'd watched for weeks while I was shooting *Top Secret!*, the same woman I had failed to approach but who had not failed to haunt me. Mind you, I had not arranged her audition. I had no idea that she was up for the part. She read with an effortless cool that made it clear to everyone she was indeed Sorsha.

So it happened. We met as peers. In the film, I would pursue her, and until late in the story, she would rebuff me. There were echoes of Kate and Petruchio in *The Taming of the Shrew*. There were also echoes of this same scenario in real life.

Willow benefited from fantastical special effects and the famous Lucas-lubricated storytelling. George was George because he was on every tiny detail, even riding lessons, which he canceled when he found out I was an excellent horseman. However, in the mountainous regions of New Zealand and Wales where we were filming, I had to ride English style, because it's all my horse knew and because we were engaging in pretty dangerous stunts. I thought lessons were crucial. At one point, I grabbed a prop in the form of a giant wooden cross, wore it on my back, and walked to the dailies theater to broach the subject. He obliged and allowed me to continue the lessons, but his look told me I had won the battle but lost the war. I wouldn't be stealing a turn as Han Solo any time soon.

My part required some athletic challenges that I enjoyed, but the character himself didn't have a lot going on. He was strong, healthy, and hopelessly romantic. I suddenly felt that I didn't have a lot going on upstairs, either. My mind and desire were concentrated exclusively on Joanne. Madmartigan has to slay a fire-breathing two-headed dragon to win Sorsha's love. Meanwhile, off-screen, I had to do even more to win Joanne's love.

It was a long six-month shoot that included time in London. Although my approach to Joanne was respectful, it was also tenacious. I was not in the least ambiguous about my feelings for her. She, in turn,

With Warwick Davis in *Willow*

was not in the least ambiguous about her feelings for me: zero interest. Thus I decided to make a move about which I am ashamed. It's the worst thing I have ever done to a woman, consciously. Every time I tell this story, I put a blanket over my head to hide my embarrassment. As you read this, please envision me with a blanket over my head.

I'd had a girlfriend who was the unequivocal ideal of beauty, an American sweetheart with a top note or whisper of exotic power. Cherry pie made with fresh rosewater. And she was a budding star.

Our romance, a sometime thing, had smoldered and simmered for quite a while.

And by the time *Willow* began shooting, she may not have still been carrying a torch for me, but she was definitely carrying a candle. I used that candle to invite her to the set of *Willow*. She willingly flew across the pond, as blushing and bright as ever. On her arrival, the cast and crew were visibly impressed. This striking starlet had come to visit me. My hope, of course, was that Joanne would be equally impressed. I regret to say—and I am also delighted to say—that she was. Regret because there's always questionable karma when manipulation succeeds. But delighted because my heart was happy. Eventually so was Joanne. The American beauty, not so much. She was crestfallen. My apologies remain ongoing, in person and in the depths of my soul's consciousness and conscience.

Madmartigan and Sorsha fell in love. So did Val and Joanne. At the wrap party, we were already wrapped up in one another's arms. Joanne is an autodidact with an astute literary sensibility. She herself contains extreme sweetness and unbridled toughness. She was once a lead singer in a post-punk band. She moves with the grace of a seasoned dancer. Madly in love, we decided to chill out in London, where Jeremy Irons lent us his flat. The *Willow* shoot had been arduous. We were bruised from the film's physical demands. Dead tired, we slept for days. Then I awoke one morning with a bright idea: "Let's clear our heads. Let's go to Africa."

Joanne's response: "Why not?"

We were still so tired, though, that we had trouble negotiating an itinerary. So we changed plans. Fly to the US, recuperate at my house in Santa Fe, and then head to Africa.

Joanne was game. I was infatuated. The brothers and their mother graciously welcomed Joanne to Santa Fe. She fell in love with the town. We covered ourselves in turquoise jewelry. We were finally clear enough to figure out an African sojourn—and off we went.

The Kenyan coast. The sky, the sea, a safari that forbade shooting, a thousand exotic birds, a thousand flighty monkeys, the elephants, the elusive eland and kudu, the mysterious leopard. People spend years searching for a glimpse of the mighty leopard, but somehow the most elusive animals just come to me.

I wanted to share everything with this woman. We set up a tent in the wilderness, its serenity broken only by the appearance, next to our cot, of a monitor lizard that had to be nine feet long, forked tongue to terrifying tail. Joanne was asleep. I thought of awakening her. I didn't want her to miss seeing this creature who possessed the physicality of a dinosaur. But I didn't want her to scream and frighten the beast into action. Approaching our cot, he was nearly tall enough to touch our faces with his forked tongue. He turned his head to examine us. I didn't move. I wasn't frozen with fear. I was frozen with awe. He inched his way out as deliberately as he'd inched his way in. After he left, I did arouse Joanne and took her outside the tent so she could see the remarkable creature slither his way into the jungle.

We slithered our way through the jungle ourselves, with guides, without guides, guileless, unafraid, afraid, excited by all we had seen and were about to see, galvanized by the unknown and the new, girded by our love, pledging that love while realizing it had to be expressed before family and friends in the form of, yes, marriage.

All this happened in about a year. We married in Santa Fe before a hundred of our friends and family members. The celebration was appropriately raucous. Outside of church, we made a private vow: that we would always be together when each of us made a movie. Otherwise, we knew the marriage would never work. Joanne's career was advancing beautifully. The following year, her role in *Scandal* as Christine Keeler, the super-sensuous English showgirl, alongside John Hurt, would win her a slew of well-merited accolades.

Though I had not yet met Brando, I arranged for our honeymoon on his island in Tahiti, which was more feral than we'd ever imagined. One night during a storm, humongous coconuts flew off trees like hail, and we had to run for our lives. It kept us laughing for a solid month. It was a scene out of *Apocalypse Now*, and our joke was that Brando, whom we never saw on the island, had commissioned the storm simply to get rid of us.

Just days after our honeymoon, Joanne went off to England to do *Scandal* and I headed out to the Colorado Shakespeare Festival, where I played the prince of Denmark. I read George Bernard Shaw, who insisted that if the actor portraying Hamlet does a single ridiculous thing, the entire production turns ridiculous—for the better. Testing that theory, seeing that Hamlet can be intimidating to the point of paralysis, I dropped my pants in front of the cast during the first day of rehearsal to present myself as willing to be nearly naked in front of them (I still had my boxers on), to be as humble as the fourth spear carrier, to show them I wasn't some Hollywood actor they couldn't make jokes about. We were a family, as all casts are, for a little while anyway.

The best play ever written is the hardest to render right. My hope was that whimsy might establish the spirit of the production by loosening up the players. My hope came true. Part of that truth was established when I encountered the only truly brilliant acting teacher I ever studied with, Peter Kass. A protégé of Clifford Odets, Peter had instructed Olympia Dukakis, Faye Dunaway, and John Cazale among so many others, and he convinced me that Hamlet was not some unapproachable towering intellect but actually pretty weak. He does what everyone in the play tells him to do, everyone from his stepfather to his vacuous school friends Rosencrantz and Guildenstern. The ghost of his father instructs him to avenge his death, and he takes about four hours to deliberate it. His equivocation, so deeply and inextricably human, is essential to his status as a flawed hero. Yet he does follow through, however against his nature it is.

I embraced that quality in Hamlet that is endemic to all human beings yet, for all our ability to think through dilemmas, can never be eradicated: confusion. I allowed Hamlet to be confused. In playing Hamlet, I allowed myself to be confused. I allowed confusion to reign. I channeled confusion so that, in a strange way, the confusion made sense.

I studied *Hamlet* for ten years before committing to it. I wanted to play him first in a place where there was no fear of national scrutiny, hence the Colorado Shakespeare Festival. I even practiced every day of my honeymoon—something Joanne was justifiably upset with, as much as she was understanding. She has a nearly photographic memory and couldn't quite grasp how I had to read the play every damn day. I tried to make it clear to her she had married a simpleton who after ten years still hadn't quite gotten the thing memorized. If you place all of Hamlet's monologues together, it's about two hours to read, depending on the delivery.

Plus, imagine how silly my Hamlet was when I was twelve, then

A promotional photo for the 1988 Colorado Shakespeare
Festival production of *Hamlet*

twenty-four, then twenty-seven. Every month nowadays it feels like
my life is completely new. Feels good. Except if I had my way my two
grown children would live downstairs and I would sleep in my living
room. I miss them every hour, even though I live so close to my daughter I can practically yell her name and she could hear me. I have to give
them their space, but I don't want to. I want to smother them and not
care that I might ruin their lives. They are my greatest joy, my proudest achievement, even though it is painfully clear I have just about zero
to do with their character. I admit it but I don't have to like it.

Where were we?

The Doors

F rench poet Arthur Rimbaud died in 1891 at age thirty-seven. American poet Jim Morrison died in 1971 at age twenty-seven. The term *enfant terrible* applies to them both. They were rebels who abused drink and drugs; they grew their hair long and scandalized society; they were consumed with the power and potential of artistic expression.

Rimbaud wrote of the "fertility of the mind and the vastness of the world." Morrison wrote, "I can become gigantic and reach the farthest things. I can change the course of nature. I can place myself anywhere in space or time."

I read Rimbaud in a book but got to play Morrison in a movie. I always connected the two. That's why when I was cast in the movie, I primarily saw myself playing a poet. My esteemed director, Oliver Stone, wrote his very first screenplay for a solid year in his New York studio apartment the moment he returned from Vietnam, a purple heart in his pocket. And who did he write that film for? Jim Morrison. Imagine how Oliver felt watching *Apocalypse Now* for the first time, hearing Coppola's brilliant choice of Morrison's brilliant tune, "The End." All about death. Probably Jim's favorite subject.

I loved making *The Doors* and working for Oliver. The truth is that I had the fight of my life ahead of me. But not for the reasons you think. Again, I worked on *Hamlet* for ten years before I felt I was ready. In the case of *The Doors*, I used every element inside me to embody this character. Unlike so many instances where I used indifference to excite a casting director's interest, this time I worked my ass off. I had no choice. Because I had a calling. I could not *not* play Morrison.

Initially Oliver pretended I wasn't quite right for the role, or perhaps he wasn't quite sure himself. He would dangle the carrot and almost torture me. He loved getting under people's skin. It was a favorite technique of his to generate or capture something real from an actor, not their prepared role, which often, it has to be said, isn't very spontaneous. I had auditioned for him before, and when I really wowed him, he would lean in and quietly say, "You know, Tom Cruise really really wants to play this part." Or Bono. Or Nic Cage. I would tease him right back: "Have fun with that." But I'd offer ideas and excitement along the way. For example, for the part of Jim I felt the actor had to sing the songs live, to have a cathartic experience that the players onstage evoke, not in advance of the audience, but with them in a moment of unique empathy. The role of the actor is to quell alienation, to recognize that in a way, we are all one.

Jim was a rare baritone-tenor, so I trained to sing in that range. I rented a studio, worked on the songs for months, and made a basement tape. My idea was simple: Present two recordings to Oliver as well as to the original members of the Doors. One tape was me singing, the other was actually Jim. My gamble was to see if Stone and the Doors could tell who was who. When the time finally came, they couldn't tell us apart. I had found my inner Jim.

Oliver was visibly moved and quietly offered me the time to record several records with the brilliant invisible fifth member of the band, the producer of all their music, Paul Rothchild. It was love at first sight. He was even more of a maniac perfectionist than me. Some of the songs weren't even in the film. We were just getting deep into the ozone of the zone. Paul got lost in the revelry and nostalgia. I got lost in the spirit of the Lizard King. Sometimes he was so technical it drove me crazy. I would be knee-deep in a primal scream and hear, "That was great, Jim, but we're going to go back to line twelve, second stanza, and clean that up a bit. Just a second while we cue it up." He really thought I was Jim at moments.

One time I was upset with a particular song. Which made Paul upset. He turned purple yelling at me down the mic in the engineer's booth. He was suffering at the time and had to have oxygen on occasion. This was one of those times.

"Stop it, Val!" he shouted. "Stop it! Stop it!"

"Hey man," I started. "Hey man" was Jim's favorite form of address, and I spoke twenty-four seven in his laconic, ironic, super slow delivery. "Hey man, all I am saying is that this song is the dumbest, worst piece of filth I ever wrote and I don't want to sing it now or ever."

"Val, I'm serious," Paul said. "Stop it. This is too much. I just can't."

He was visibly upset, and started to shake and weep. He went outside, past my recording booth. I immediately followed and apologized in the best Val voice I could muster.

"I'm really sorry, Paul. I won't talk in his dialect anymore. It's just there's so little time and for me the best way is just—"

"No, no, no," Paul said. "It's not that. It's . . . it's . . . it's what you are saying. I don't know who told you those things about the song but he said them only to me, and I've never told anyone. So I just need you to stop it for a while."

As Jim Morrison

It was impossible for me to convince Paul of the utter truth of the situation, but I had always had a knack for this crazy job of mine, and somehow, through all the months and months of studying Jim, his interviews and video, and talking to his friends and reading all his girls' manuscripts about their time with him, somehow I was able to like the same things he liked—or in this particular case didn't like—in a poet or a band or even his own writing, as Paul was now freaking out about. I was torturing Paul with the exact words Jim had used all those years ago when they recorded the song that one and only day he ever sang it. And no, I'm not ever going to tell you which song it was. What if it's your favorite? Where will that get us? I will say it's none of their zillion top-ten hits. It's a pretty crap song. Just accept it. I was right. Jim was right.

I told Paul to take all the time he needed, and I'd walk down the street to visit a friend of mine and be back soon. This guy I knew was a massive cokehead and happened to live near the studio. The drugs got to be too much for me to be around so I never saw this guy anymore, but he was a real smart guy and knew rock and roll really well so it was a timely meeting. When I returned, I applied some of what he told me about Jim's amazing presence onstage, and I said to Paul, "Do me a favor and put up 'The End.'"

Paul took a very long time, out of respect for me as an artist, to tell me he just wasn't going to do that. We had avoided it forever. I just couldn't sing it. It was too difficult. I grew more and more assertive, and assured him that I really didn't mind how badly I sang it—a lie—but I just really needed to for my growth as a character, and it was the best way to move past our earlier fight. Finally, he agreed, and as God is my witness, Paul cried even harder after I had finished. He stopped recording and came into the booth and hugged me for the longest time. We both sat on the floor. As a producer, he had always given notes instantly and immediately and demand the artist follow his instructions to the absolute letter. So this was really weird, this break in his professionalism. Finally, he became settled enough to explain. He looked at me with a look I will never forget. And he said, in a whisper, "That was perfect, Val. Perfect. Just perfect. Except for two places. And I swear to God, those are the same two places Jim messed up. That's why there are two takes of that song, rather than punching-in." Which is slang for when a producer has an artist record a portion of a song rather than having them record the whole song over again, because it is near impossible to record a flawless track unless you are a mad genius like David Bowie, famous for his one-take masterpieces, or John Lennon or Bob Dylan or Bruce Springsteen, artists who grew up playing live so recording "live" is second nature to them.

Well, I got chills like I never had them before during my time playing Jim. So far I had been shocked many times by how I was able to sing way beyond my talent or range. Especially challenging were Jim's screams–those primal screams which Jim did better than just about anyone and which I practiced endlessly. But that whole day just seemed to have had a lot of Jim floating around Paul and me. So there were two grown men sitting on the dusty floor of a recording studio near Melrose reduced to tears because of Jim Morrison's prophetic psalm to himself about dying. Not saving it for the end of his career but beginning with it, just so that there would be no doubt in the listener's mind. "Can you picture what will be / so limitless and free." I can. I did.

People assumed I took drugs to emulate Jim's state of mind. I did the opposite. I stayed super clean, jogging ten miles a day. To get into Jim's cloudy mind, I required absolute clarity. My routine was physical exertion during the day and Morrison music at night. I also built what are called tailor's mirrors, enabling you to see three floor-to-head images of yourself all at once, so you can take a glance at your left side while favoring your right. I focused on how Jim would appear from all camera angles. I had to master his look, as he was so familiar to so many fans.

Yet while I very much cared about the verisimilitude of appearance, I was just as focused on channeling his soul, took hold of him from the inside out, from the ribs. The story to me was Jim's glory and then his demise, the Greek fleet waiting to sail him into his fate, to die with rock and roll in one mighty catastrophe. Jester, warrior, performer. Maybe, if I tried hard enough, I could break through and reflect his light, free his mind, and, through some Bacchanalian surge of prowess, offer healing to myself, to Jim and everyone watching.

With this in mind, I offered an approach to Oliver. I thought there was more to the story than the basic idea of sex, drugs, and rock and roll. I thought it crucial to represent Jim as a true poet whose forefather was Rimbaud and, through Rimbaud, the Beat poets Ferlinghetti, Ginsberg, and Corso. Before Rimbaud was William Blake, the mystic eighteenth-century poet who wrote in *The Marriage of Heaven and Hell*, "If the doors of perception were cleansed, everything would appear to man as it is: infinite." Aldous Huxley borrowed Blake's phrase—"the doors of perception"—for the title of his book about psychedelics. I felt we needed desperately to dramatize how deeply Jim wrestled with words, in much the same way as John Keats, he, too, a poet overwhelmed by beauty yet obsessed with the need to express it, a poet whose early death at age twenty-five in some ways mirrored Jim's. Why is it that poets feel this need to connect with their ancestors? Is it that we all must identify with a tribe?

I lobbied Oliver about including some scenes which I hoped would reveal Jim as a serious poet trying to figure out his life through his religion—art—and he made many changes to accommodate my commitment. He and I adore each other, and more than a decade later we would work together again on *Alexander*. But perhaps I lacked the wisdom to understand that creativity, like prayer for me, is best expressed without insistence or force. I understand actors who want to be considered "easy to work with." Actors don't want day jobs. Actors want to act. Gaining a reputation as a cooperative thespian is not a bad thing. I do not condemn my brothers and sisters who have developed personalities pleasing to directors. I have, in fact, pleased dozens of directors. Others I have not. And when I have not, it isn't through ego. It's simply because I have connected with a character and must honor that connection. How to do that is an ongoing lesson, and despite our debates and differences, working with such a brilliant director as Oliver on such a profound subject as The Doors was something I hope to remember in many, many lifetimes.

The members of the band appreciated my performance, which was tremendous affirmation. And some argue it remains the best rock

With Oliver Stone on the set of *The Doors*

and roll film ever made. I don't know how you say what's best. It's all so personal. Though I will say back then wasn't like it is now, with all the billion-dollar music biopic hits. Back then, Hollywood for some reason looked down on them. While I don't know if I have ever done it all the way like others have done it for me—Toshiro Mifune in *Yojimbo*, say, or those moments of genius in Chaplin, or metamorphoses from contemporaries such as Robert Downey Jr. in *Tropic Thunder*, Cate Blanchett in *Elizabeth*, Meryl Streep in *Sophie's Choice*, Sean Penn in *Milk*, Joaquin Phoenix in *The Master*, Hilary Swank in *Boys Don't Cry*, Rooney Mara in the American version of *The Girl with the Dragon Tattoo*, and Viola Davis in everything, just to name a few—I see my work in *The Doors* as one of the proudest moments of my career. That's because I was praying with my poetic ancestors in real time, and because of Oliver's generosity of spirit and our mutual respect for something Jim held sacred: a magical moment onstage. When it happens, we all feel the unity of spirit.

Shattered

After *The Doors*, I took a year off and left Hollywood and didn't even read a script for seven months. My agent fairly pulled her hair out that I didn't stay in Los Angeles and lobby for an award. She tried to get me to see how my performance was something many people in our industry wanted to acknowledge, perhaps even reward my effort with a statue. But I always figured that if my work was good enough it didn't require beating a drum about it. And besides, I had more important things to focus on.

At the beginning of the Jim Morrison saga, Joanne surprised me with an announcement. She had been offered a part in *Shattered* with Tom Berenger, Greta Scacchi, and Bob Hoskins. The film was being shot in San Francisco. She wanted to accept.

I didn't have to remind her that our marriage vow prevented this. We had pledged to be together during every movie, knew the hundreds of ways that filmmaking eats away at a romance if you are both working. I obviously couldn't leave *The Doors*. I had already put body and soul into it. We were about to start shooting. I wanted her to stay with me and asked her to decline the offer. She wouldn't. I was hurt but not angry. I don't know at what point you stop hurting and start healing. Joanne is a talented and ambitious actor. Ambitious myself, I'd have been a fool not to understand. This was early in her career. Good roles are hard to come by. There was no reason my career should have come before hers. There was no big scene. She left, and I continued my work as Jim.

I've never said this out loud or written it down before, but I was on edge, anxious and almost terrified because I could feel Joanne slipping away. And perhaps it was because I, too, was slipping away that I'd have visions of her falling for our friends, like the sensuous, quietly mischievous Liam Neeson, who Joanne had done a film with. Liam was like a modern Gregory Peck, who felt to both of us like the ideal man, a perfect cocktail of the stoic man's man Gary Cooper, who had a sense of humor about his good fortune, and the paradigm of a suave film star like Clark Gable. I remember wondering if she would fall for him. He was awfully charming. Those damn Irishmen! They say the reason you feel jealousy is because you yourself may be entertaining a questionable agenda. All possible, and yet my premonitions remained strong.

The thing I kept thinking of was the film she was about to make: *Shattered*. Mind you, this was before the birth of Mercedes and Jack, our two beautiful children. Years of happiness lay before us. Years of conflict as well. The dance between darkness and light would continue. I do believe, though, that it was during those light-dark days of *The Doors* that, when Joanne understandably took her departure, I knew in my heart that our marriage would not last. I ascribe fault to no one. I now see it as a matter of fate. And who was I but the partner who went away literally for half the day sometimes on our honeymoon? What planet was I on? How could I expect her to be supportive about such heartlessness? Nonetheless, I loved being married. And soon I would love having children.

But now I was dealing with the blues that come after a film is finished. It's a postpartum blues. Artists can become severely depressed when they're not performing. What is this business of giving our bodies and souls over to magic so mercilessly that we have nothing left for ourselves? Is it God or the devil? Maybe my postpartum, post-*Doors* blues came from a deep knowledge. Maybe I feared no project would ever be quite as special. I felt like I had experienced glory. Nirvana. And what next? To live or die? What would life look like, pretending to be normal after getting a taste of heaven? After touching the pearly gates?

Fortunately, someone would then enter my life who no doubt understood these feelings all too well and could offer a sympathetic ear and advice. A legend. A hero. And soon enough a friend.

Brando

After I shot *The Doors* and Joanne shot *Shattered*, we flew off to Ireland to wind down and reconnect. I've always seen Ireland as a literary land—George Bernard Shaw, William Butler Yeats, James Joyce, Samuel Beckett—and find solace in its charming cities and cool green countryside. Much of the tension my wife and I had experienced in the past year seemed to melt under the summer sun.

Back in Santa Fe, a friend called to say Marlon Brando wanted to meet me. My heart broke into a happy song. Apparently he had seen *The Doors* and was curious.

I rode to his home on Mulholland Drive in a state of high excitement. A young Russian writer on his way to meet Tolstoy. A young German composer about to jam with Bach. A young boxer off to spar with Ali.

I arrived early and was shown to his den filled with artifacts—Native American art, a set of bongo drums, books of every variety, all in casual disarray. I waited for over an hour. I was eager but necessarily patient. I figured this was part of the ritual. I felt fortunate. I dug the ritual.

The door opened and Marlon slowly walked through. His face was covered with makeup. It was as though he were in whiteface. He wore a white muumuu that covered his enormous frame. He was as big as a grand piano. He was as big as Orson Welles. He sat in an oversize easy chair. I sat on a couch in front of him.

His first question was, "I was wondering if you're familiar with the work of Paul Muni."

I knew Muni was considered one of the great actors of the thirties and forties but could only remember seeing him in *The Last Angry Man*.

"Not as familiar as I probably need to be," I said.

"Are you too young to remember John Garfield?"

"I've heard it said that Garfield was Brando before Brando was Brando."

Brando liked that remark.

"What about Buster Keaton?"

"Yes."

"Do you know his work well?" asked Marlon.

"I could know it better."

"And Gene Hackman, of course. Gene Hackman is the actor's actor."

Saying that, Marlon's lips turned up ever so slightly at their edges.

He began speaking of other actors he admired—Edward G. Robinson, Karl Malden, Jean-Paul Belmondo. He mentioned Lino Ventura, who starred in Jean-Pierre Melville's *Army of Shadows*, the classic film about the French Resistance. He didn't say anything about *The Doors*. He didn't even indicate that he had seen it. But I had the feeling—although it may be my ego—that in discussing good actors he was including me in that company. Or at least I wasn't made to feel excluded.

During one long pause I found the courage to ask him, "What do you think of Samuel Beckett?"

I've had a lifelong fascination with Beckett's work and was curious to hear Brando's point of view. His response shocked me.

"I've never read him."

"But you've seen his plays."

"Not one."

"I'm surprised."

"Why?"

"Well, because . . . Samuel Beckett is so seminal."

"Perhaps. Perhaps if I read him, I would agree. But I haven't. Of all the world's literature, none of us have read more than a fraction of the great works. What do we know of the literature of Indonesia? There are surely poets, playwrights, and novelists in Iceland and Haiti who merit our attention."

Of course I agreed with this but wondered whether Marlon was telling the truth about Beckett. He had come of age in the theater when Beckett was all the rage. It was hard to believe he'd never seen a single performance of *Waiting for Godot*. I also wondered whether, because he had chosen not to act in a Beckett play, he avoided the subject by claiming not to know his work. Or maybe he just wanted to shock me with an answer I never expected.

He seemed pleased to see me shocked. I didn't mind. I was just so happy to be in a room with Marlon Brando. From there, the conversation eased up. I was able to express my appreciation of his craft. I didn't at all resist sounding like a fanboy. I spoke of two of my favorite Brando lines: when as Kid Rio in *One Eyed Jacks* he calls his adversary a "scum-sucking pig," and the monumental mutiny scene in *Mutiny on the Bounty*, when, as Fletcher Christian, he slaps his superior Captain Bligh (played by Trevor Howard) and says, in his gloriously understated English accent, "You bloody bastard! You'll not put your foot on me again."

"Do you have a list of your own favorite lines?" Brando asked in return.

I admitted that I did not.

"Neither do I. I'd rather not remember."

"Even something as grand as *Last Tango in Paris*?"

He spoke about that experience ruefully. He had good things to say about director Bernardo Bertolucci—did I know he was also a fine poet who grew up in the communist-dominated city of Parma, Italy?—but did not want to discuss Paul, the character he portrayed. "The pain borne by that peculiar man," he said, "became a burden I carried for far too long."

"As actors, how do we free ourselves of all those post-production burdens?"

Marlon's answer came swiftly. "We don't."

We spoke all afternoon. Although we all indulge in gossip, Marlon had a strict rule: if you weren't present for someone's remark, he refused to hear the comment. Firsthand accounts only. Beyond an occasional anecdote about certain directors he admired or disliked, the gist of the conversation was Marlon, in his offhanded way, suggesting certain movies I might see and books I might read. He assumed an avuncular attitude. Great. I wanted Marlon Brando to be my uncle, my friend, my anything. He liked to speak in riddles. He valued ambiguity over clarity. Yet for all his eagerness to respond to my questions in ways that he hoped I'd find puzzling, there was a certain warmth about him. I presumed he'd invite me back, and he did.

Thinking over my initial meeting with Brando, I now realize that the makeup and muumuu had a certain irony I missed the first time around. He was taking on the role of a great man, a great actor, while at the same time mocking that role. There was also the chance he had just finished doing an on-camera interview. But he did wear makeup often, so I suppose he had some vanity attached to his aging skin.

I met Marlon when he was in his sixties, and he was still having kids left and right like a Catholic teenager newly married after World War II. Just remarkable. How many children did he have altogether? I am not sure and am tempted to Google. I almost never Google people. I would like to live learning the old-fashioned way, if that's even possible. I don't know what I am intending by that comment. Life is moving so exponentially fast, it is just about impossible to imagine those thirty years ago when I first met Marlon, that time just before this heart-stopping, heart-stomping technological era which we can never undo. Certainly it is possible to just not respond to texts or emails, but I admit when my iPhone is out of reach I start to get a little antsy in a way that, I know from playing so many addicts, is a physical feeling very close to chemical dependence. Boy, do I pray about that often—the idea of needing some physical thing more than the unity of the spirit, more than the principles of mind, soul, life, truth, Love.

Now I, too, am officially in my sixties. Every time I speak, I must put a finger to the aperture in my throat to be understood. Cher says that I remain adorable but Cher says that to lots of guys. But like Brando, my body has taken on a much different form. Also like Brando, I choose to accept this form with equanimity.

Confusions & Contradictions

I now invoke the protection of the great gray-bearded poet of the nineteenth century whose queer sensibility speaks to all humanity with tender Love and rare wisdom. Walt Whitman's famous answer to the self-imposed question "Do I contradict myself?" was "Very well then I contradict myself, / (I am large, I contain multitudes.)"

I'd amend that to include an additional question: "Am I confused? Yes, I embrace confusion." All this is a lead-up to a statement I must make about making movies.

Going through my filmography, my first reaction is that these films have nothing to do with my life. My second reaction is that they have everything to do with my life.

I am none of the characters I have portrayed, and I am all of the characters. Good acting requires both detachment and engagement—and, most of all, nonjudgment. Playing a character means detaching myself from whatever preconceived notions I might have of them. It requires that I conduct research, much as a scientist researches a specimen. Except that the specimen needs to be brought back to life as a living, breathing human being replete with contradictions and confusions. To overwhelm the contradictions and confusions with clichés is a crime against nature. The commitment to character requires an open heart. I must allow myself to feel deeply. Such feelings linger—for weeks or hours or even a lifetime. Thus at the end of the film I carry that character somewhere in my soul. Just as I am a composite of all my characters, each character I've played is a composite of me. I don't know, though, how to break down that composite.

I do know that virtually every film or play I've acted in has been difficult—some even torturous—because of the fact that I am not in control. I realize the deficits of control. I know control can stifle one's soul. I know that to surrender to the universe, to follow a divine plan not of one's own making, is spiritually sound. To an alarming degree, the need to control comes out of fear. Yet in the context of art, the artist's relationship to the control of his/her environment is complex. I both do and do not want my character to control me. And I both do and do not want to control my character. Moreover, my inability to control the overall context in which my character is operating is often maddening. It could be the script; it could be the director or the producer. If they see the story one way and my character sees it another way, conflict is inevitable. At times conflict yields exciting art. Other times it yields lousy art. One of the reasons that early on I learned to love writing so fervently is because in writing such conflicts don't exist. Or if they do, I can voice them—which is exactly what I'm doing right now—so the reader might possibly benefit from my uncertainty.

There are lots of reasons to make art, but I usually migrate toward the educational aspect of it. I like to learn from art. It's almost impossible for me to learn in any formal way, yet I love to learn. I love that about the Jewish culture and faith: knowledge is holy, learning is holy. Oh how glorious! Brando used to be so eloquent about his being really turned on about formal study from his introduction to the Jewish community through Stella Adler and that original bunch from the Actors Studio. He even lived at her house for a time and had an affair with her daughter. I can't recall if he told Stella about that. He also claimed to have had an affair with Jackie Kennedy in the kitchen of the White House. And that from a guy who said he hated gossip. He never hated gossiping about the ladies, that I ever saw.

A big part of me says, "Consider my life outside the realm of my public work." I like the way that statement sounds. And I may make it again before this story is over. But I don't trust those words entirely. Which is why I have no choice but to continue the difficult task of locating the nexus where my life and my art meet. Wish me luck.

Thunderheart

I t was my good fortune to act in the film *Thunderheart*. In reading the script, I recognized my character, Ray Levoi, as a man struggling to find himself. I was doubly attracted to the role because Ray's father was a Native American and Ray had rejected his Native American identity. The film dramatizes his struggle to regain his identity. A straitlaced government agent who has indifference and even contempt for his Native American heritage, Ray learns to embrace it. It's a murder mystery unfolding on a Lakota reservation, but also a hero's journey to which I related: moving from safe and familiar ground to divine consciousness.

Director Michael Apted had just prior to our film done a documentary, narrated by Robert Redford, *Incident at Oglala*, about two FBI agents who had been shot at the Pine Ridge reservation. *Thunderheart* drew on that troubling episode as well as the Wounded Knee occupation in the seventies, which underscored the repeated injustices suffered by Native Americans.

I was also pleased and honored because this, in the early nineties, was to be the inaugural film from TriBeCa, the newly formed production house run by Robert De Niro and Jane Rosenthal. Uninvited, I was always writing and rewriting roles in movies, my own roles and roles for others. After reading *Thunderheart*, I wrote a part in the film for Brando.

I thought back to high school, when I watched the 1973 Academy Awards live broadcast from the Dorothy Chandler Pavilion in downtown Los Angeles. Liv Ullmann and Roger Moore announced that Marlon Brando had won best actor for *The Godfather*. But Brando didn't accept the award. He refused to attend. In his place he sent to the podium the radiant Sacheen Littlefeather, an Apache actress and activist who, with great poise, announced that Brando was rejecting the Oscar in protest of our treatment of Native Americans. Some booed. Others heckled. Later that evening Clint Eastwood joked while presenting the Best Picture award that he was doing so on behalf of all the cowboys shot in John Ford films. He saw Marlon's ploy as a joke. I saw it as heroism.

Marlon was my guy. It wasn't about being flawlessly eloquent like Laurence Olivier or John Gielgud. It wasn't about being suave like Cary Grant or homespun like Gary Cooper. It was about the power of silence. The long, pregnant pause. The understatement. The boiling subtext. The unexpressed. The mystery. The mumbling. Trying as we all do in life to make sense of a moment. The rage that remains inside. The penetrating look. Eyes slightly shifting. Lips slightly curling. The beauty of subterfuge.

That same year Marlon told the Academy to screw themselves, he came on a TV talk show where host Dick Cavett asked him why he had so often belittled the art of acting. Brando's unexpected retort still serves to keep me sane. "We couldn't survive a second," he said, "if we weren't able to act . . . acting is a survival mechanism . . . we act to save our lives."

Well, in the year of *Thunderheart*, I was set to save Marlon. Like so many of us, he had suffered financial setbacks. He needed cash, and I was determined to rush to his rescue. Given his passion for indigenous people, I knew he'd be perfect as the crusading head of the FBI. I worked for weeks writing and rewriting scenes for Marlon. I polished the dialogue to a high gleam. I really pushed it with De Niro, whom I considered a friend. Despite his extreme need for privacy, Bob had let me into his perfectionist world. I begged him to read the scenes I had custom-crafted for Brando. I sent Bob notes. I called him dozens of times, until the day of reckoning. I was on the phone with Bob, passionately arguing how Brando could transform this film. Bob is always silent, but this time he was so stone silent. Finally, he uttered the words:

"Val," he said emphatically, "Marlon Brando. Is. Not. Going. To. Be. In this movie."

As aggravating as it was not to play beside Brando, it was thrilling to play beside Sam Shepard, who wrote as well as he acted and did both with a natural ease that turns me green with envy. The envy never lasted long because I loved Sam. I loved him for his adventurous spirit, his big heart, and inventive mind. I miss him every day of my life. In *Thunderheart*, Sam and I played complicated characters. I could—and did—spend lots of time talking about all this with Sam. I can easily get wrapped up in character dissection. It's fun. And in doing character analysis, I admit, I am not immune to falling in love with my analysis. Not so with Sam. Sam wasn't a talker. He was a thinker, a drinker, a homespun yet sophisticated philosopher, but was never in love with the sound of his own voice. Fewer words, the better.

With Sam Shepard in *Thunderheart*

One late evening in the middle of production he had had enough of my ponderous overthinking.

"It goes like this, Val," he said. "I'm the bad guy. You're the good guy."

That shut me up but good. The film was shot in South Dakota on the Lakota reservation. I went to many ceremonies and became friends for life with many beautiful families. I made it clear I had to be home by summer's end. That's because I was going to be a father. One of the most glorious moments of my life was about to unfold.

Colic Convulsion
Then Holy Miracle

L ike millions of others, Joanne and I began reading *What to Expect When You're Expecting* the moment we learned she was pregnant. I wanted to know everything. I did not want to be like one of those dads banished before the birth of their baby who wind up at bars or brothels or tobacco shops buying cigars for their cronies. I wanted to study the process, and I also did not want to know the sex. We wanted to relish the unknown of every single day of gestation. I also thought it was important that my normally fit body not be fit at all. I decided to gain weight, not to equal Joanne's weight, but at least enough to engender empathy. What's it like to have your body radically change? What does that do to your head and your heart and your sense of self?

Joanne and I both felt a home birth with a midwife was perfect for our rustic lifestyle.

The problem was that the midwife didn't really like me. It was a moment when I saw the growing imbalance in our marriage. My desire to be a dad was all-consuming, yet that desire went unrecognized.

I nonetheless inserted myself into this gestation period with joyous intensity. The closer we came to the birth, the more excited we grew.

October 1991. The final weeks. We had moved from my original rented quarters in Tesque, an extremely beautiful little suburb just outside the city limits of Santa Fe to our very first home, its ample grounds within earshot of the city's famous outdoor opera venue. In the distance, we could almost make out Verdi or Puccini wafting in over the summer breeze. The air was chilled and the earth blanketed in snow when Joanne's water broke. I figured this was it. Except it wasn't. The midwife said that yes, labor had begun, but labor could well linger a long while. Some women lie down. Some women eat; some bathe in warm water. Joanne wanted to walk. Walking, she felt, would facilitate things. Oh, did we walk! Walked for one day, then a second, then a third. Even as contractions ensued, we kept walking. Walking miles and miles. Joanne was intrepid, almost to a fault. On the third day of our walking routine, we went to the stable that was part of our compound, where, coincidentally, Apple, Joanne's favorite horse, was colicking. With all four legs, she kicked at her stomach. Joanne knew instantly her horse was in danger of dying. Alarmed for her horse, Joanne ran over to her. Alarmed for my wife and our child, I ran over to Joanne. It was hell pulling her away from the manic horse, but I managed. The horse's distress had thrown Joanne into a state of delirium. I called a vet and the horse was eventually saved, which was a great relief to us both.

Back at the house, nearing the end of three days of intense labor, walking what felt like could have been twenty miles during contractions, I dropped the home-birth plan and decided to drive Joanne to the hospital. Ms. Midwife said no. I had to get right up in her grill and make it plain she was not the boss in our home. She followed us to the hospital. I managed to get Joanne into a four-wheel drive. Now, the snow was coming down in sheets, but I was prepared. I knew the regular roads could become impassable and had the back roads mapped out. We made it. Our baby was born. I was the first to hold her. I cut the cord. We wept. Our Mercedes! Precious angel, gift of God. We knew our lives would be changed, our capacities for Love expanded. When I asked the nurse where my bed was, she thought I was kidding. Apparently no new dad had ever made such a request. After a few hours, she brought me up a piece of old foam rubber and a used blanket. I slept on the linoleum floor.

And though I tried to get in there—to change and bathe the baby, to cuddle and kiss her and sing sweet lullabies in her tiny ear—it was as though this was women's work. My maternal instincts were manifesting like crazy but so often had to be suppressed. In the end, I did become a hands-on and adoring dad, but never to the degree I desired. But I have faith. I am still trying to be the best dad I can be.

Doc Holidays

I'm proud of the work I did on *Billy the Kid*, a made-for-TV Western written by Gore Vidal, the towering member of the literati. In thinking about the role, I may have had in mind Brando's Kid Rio, the hero of the only movie Marlon ever directed, *One Eyed Jacks*. That film was made when I was an infant. When I was an adult and Brando's friend, he told me that at some point every film actor must make a Western. When I asked him why, he answered with his famous half smile and the words, "You know damn well why."

I presume the *why* has to do with basic Americanism. One way or the other, Americans have to deal with the West and its glorious, sordid, and sadistic past. Marlon knew that the West represents both our territorial salvation and our mortal sin, our gain and our greed. We fought lawlessness to create an even more lawless law, one that excused and perpetuated genocide. Even today, this gun-obsessed nation that we love remains enmired in a dilemma centered on pistols and rifles with romantic ties to our murderous past. We love Westerns. We learn everything from Westerns and yet learn nothing from them.

We continue killing ourselves in unconscionable ways. The archetype of the gunslinger, played with a naturalism that only Brando could invoke, is ever present. I could never give up the chance to play such a character. That's why when I had the chance to play Doc Holliday, I grabbed it.

I've entitled this tome *I'm Your Huckleberry* for many reasons. I like the unintentional echo of *Huckleberry Finn*, which is my favorite novel and features my favorite character. I also realize that the line that I, playing the diseased Doc Holliday, articulated has become iconic. I speak it before shooting to death the fearsome Johnny Ringo, played by Michael Biehn. By the way, despite some fans' contention that in the 1800s the handles of caskets were called *huckles* and thus the word *huckle bearer* was a term for *pall bearer*, I do not say, "I'm your huckle bearer." I say, "I'm your huckleberry," connotating, "I'm your man. You've met your match."

In trying to understand the character of Doc Holliday, it's important to remember he's a fallen aristocrat, frustrated by his inability to express his authentic self. His greatest retribution for this loss was his caustic wit. His tongue is more lethal than his pistol. Throughout the drama, he's dying of both drink and tuberculosis. In playing him, I thought of what my dear friend the great screenplay writer Robert Towne had taught me: all insightful dialogue comes out of situations, not predeveloped thought. In that regard, I saw Doc's situation as dire. I also saw his action as defiance in the face of death. I loved him.

My castmates were wonderful—Kurt Russell as Wyatt Earp, and Sam Elliott and Bill Paxton as his brothers—and the experience was profound. I had read only half of Kevin Jarre's brilliant screenplay before I made up my mind to accept the role. That's happened only two other times in my career (with *Batman* and *Kiss Kiss Bang Bang*). When

With Kurt Russell as Wyatt Earp and Doc Holliday

I take on a part, I usually read the script many times before reciting a word out loud.

I was especially attuned to the rhythms of Doc's speech, so much so that I called Kevin with the most specific of questions. I said, "There's a comma on page thirty-two where I don't think Doc needs to pause. Wouldn't it be more effective if he simply drew out the line?"

"When you get more into the drawl," said Kevin, "you'll find that the pause is right."

"Are you certain?"

"I am," said Kevin. He was. And he was in no mood to argue about a comma. The fact that Kevin proved to be right—the comma was necessary to that musicality—shows that sometimes the writer hears his creation with greater acuity than the actor. Sometimes.

Rehearsals were hilarious. There were five or six actors who had played leads in blockbusters. Many times very small parts seemed to become what the whole film was about.

Fortunately, my wife and daughter were on set. Our little girl glowed; she was radiant and adorable and won the hearts of the entire crew. Everyone wanted to play with Mercedes. All went well until the first day of shooting. Moments of mystical wonderment morphed into a filmmaking fiasco.

Kurt Russell and I were on horses. Horses are always tricky. They want to move. They do move. Even super-skilled riders like me and Kurt had to listen to the whims of our steeds, and this day they were trying to tell us something. Writer Kevin Jarre was directing. Before Kevin said, "Action," I looked up and saw a bald eagle flying straight to the heavens holding a rattlesnake in his talons. In midflight, another magnificent bald eagle snatched the slithering snake. Both eagles flew higher and higher, passing the rattler back and forth in a rare mating dance. I was stunned. I was moved. It was a moment of glory—like a total eclipse of the sun. It had origins in the folklore of Native Americans. In the green, white, and red flag of Mexico an eagle sitting upon a prickly pear has a rattlesnake ensnared in its talons. The eagle is strength, the sacred snake is knowledge, the pear is life itself. The symbolism of what I had been blessed to witness was overwhelming.

And then Kevin Jarre shouted, "Action!" The problem was, there was no shot. Kevin had positioned the camera at an untenable angle. It seemed to me that Kevin, great writer though he was, didn't know much about directing. Kurt looked me straight in the eye and said, "Val, we're in trouble." I had to say something. I did, as gently as possible, but there was no way my remarks didn't reveal Kevin's ineptitude. He didn't last long. Blockbuster director George Cosmatos was

On set with Mercedes

brought in. Dozens of cast and crew members were canned. It was an unholy mess. I teamed up with Kurt to edit long sections of the script, because the studio couldn't give us any more time or money and we were already a month into shooting, which we now had to make up for. It's amazing the film turned out as well as it did.

I cherish the experience of working with Kurt, whom I love like a brother. When the Academy widens their awards to include something like the lifetime achievement award for Best, Most Unique, Lovely Person for Decades in a Row, if Kurt isn't the first recipient, I'll eat my Doc Holliday hat. The film has a cult following, as does my beloved Doc. And though I ducked under the radar of major Hollywood nods of approval, I got a tip of the hat from the golden prince of the West himself, Mr. Bob Dylan.

I'd known Bob since a mutual friend introduced us, right after *The Doors*. I ran into him in London when he was hanging with Ronnie Wood, a hell of a talent and free spirit I've known and loved forever. When Bob saw me, he turned and, like a laser printer, spat out the funniest line I had ever heard about *The Doors*:

"Hey . . . I hear you did that thing about that guy . . ."

And I said, "Yes, I am now fiddling with your world as well," referring to the many offers I had to cut my own record after singing every song in the film live.

Bob shot back as soon as I said *fiddle*—and you have to imagine his completely unique voice and delivery–"What, oh you playing the fiddle now, is that what you said?" He glanced like an impish genius child to Ronnie for rock icon reinforcement.

"No, no," I replied. "I mean I am messing around with music now. Might make a record."

Bob smiled. "'Cause you know fiddling . . . that's a tough road to hoe, man. Fiddling. Lots of competition."

Bob is absolutely driven. A hurricane of intense, quiet energy. If you want to know who he is at the moment, listen to how he interprets his songs at a concert today, and you'll see his soul.

Well, years later, I was in New York with my wife and little angel Mercedes and heard Bob was in town, so I called him. For some reason we were being put up by Warner Bros. at the swanky Pierre on Fifth. Not our style at all. Bob was across town in a hip, discreet hotel when he picked up. Hard to describe the thrill of hearing his voice and literally feeling his rhythm.

"Hey, man, that Doc Holliday . . ."

I couldn't believe it. Then . . . then he tried to be me as Doc. "Why, Johnny Ringo, you look like someone just walked over your grave." And then he giggled. I don't know if there's footage of his giggle but there's plenty of him smirk-laughing, and it's worth the price of admission.

I responded, "Yeah, it was a lot of fun. The writer laid it all out there for me. But thank you. What brings you to New York, Bob?"

"I'm recording an Elvis song for a charity thing with Eric Clapton and Sheryl Crow."

"Have you picked a song yet?"

"A couple. You want to come by, Val?"

"Love to."

"You're a daisy if you do!" Bob chirped back.

"What are you doing right now?"

"Nothing, doing nothing." More glorious laughter.

"You're welcome to come here, Bob. We're at the Pierre. Under the name of . . ."

"Doc Holliday. Wyatt, you're an oak. I'm your huckleberry."

I hung up blushing and whispered to my wife, "I'm not sure this isn't a dream, but I think Bob Dylan is on his way here."

Joanne is extremely hard to impress. She was impressed. She said, "That's something. How?"

"He loves Doc Holliday."

In what felt like five minutes, the doorbell rang, and Bob was on the other side in a pin-striped Western jacket. He whispered, "Ain't you gonna say nothin' from that movie?"

"Sure, right after you sing me 'Blowin' in the Wind.'"

Why did I say that?!

Maybe I was nervous.

Maybe I was starstruck.

Or maybe I just wanted him to think I was cool.

Anyway, Bob, I haven't given up on the dream of a retake.

Call me.

True Romance

During this same period it was certainly a strange gift to be cast as Elvis in Tony Scott's hyperviolent *True Romance*. The enthusiastic Tony, who had won my heart when he directed me in *Top Gun*, was set to film a script written by Quentin Tarantino. I was hoping to see Quentin on set, but he wasn't around much. He was off writing another script. *True Romance* was his first major motion picture screenplay and a breakthrough in his career. Less so for me. The idea was that the lead, Christian Slater, required a mentor. Christian's straight character idolized Elvis to the point where he said, "If I had to f——a guy, I mean had to, if my life depended on it, I'd f——Elvis."

As it turned out, I was cast as Elvis. But not only was I not f——d, I was barely seen. In this film, Elvis's face would never appear. And he was not to be called Elvis. His name was Mentor. Priscilla had given her tentative approval but ultimately pulled out because of the violence in the film. Though I dressed in Elvis costumes and assumed Elvis's trademark twang, I only popped in for short, faceless appearances when Christian needed moral support. Would I have preferred to don my guitar, shake my pelvis, and break into "Blue Suede Shoes"? Hell yes. But a shadow Elvis is better than no Elvis at all. So I thank Tony Scott and remain grateful for the chance to play, in whatever form, the forever King.

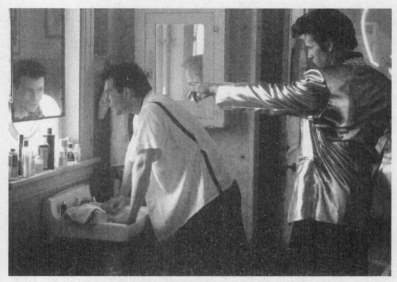

With Christian Slater in *True Romance*

ALL & SIMPLE

I'll tell you a deep secret
If you let me pull your pigtails
OK then I used to climb in my daddy's T-shirt
Up to the tree-house eucalyptus
And jump a little-boy air balloon but I'd land Jesus
I'd jump with my little white arms stretched out wide
And when I landed in the sand I'd be Jesus and love everyone &
Everything the same all & simple every thought and every dream
From my ugly math teacher to the tiny sunbeam glinting through the
Eucalyptus feathers & I'd bless the bark & trunk and I'd have a
Beard & long hair & take off my little-boy Jockey underwear &
Climb again & jump clean and whole as Jesus years ago
Jesus in my robe of Daddy's underclothes
Flying towards Damascus

—Ware, England, 1987

Eugene D. Kilmer

I t was 1993. I was in New Mexico pursuing what I then thought was my masterpiece, an African film called simply *Africa* that I intended to cowrite, produce, and direct. I was working with Bernard Pomerance, the poet and playwright whose credits included *The Elephant Man*. When it came to script conferences, Bernard was maniacally prompt. Knowing that, it was madness for me to take my daily horse ride, as I couldn't possibly make it back on time. But I was obsessed lately with finding a trail that led to a peak I could see from my ranch. To my good and bad fortune, I discovered this trail I had long been searching for. I made the climb; dismounted CJ, a horse I adored more than anything I had ever owned; tied him off and took in the spectacular view; then, at the rim of a bowl, sat in prayer for my father, who was, after all, the man who had led me to New Mexico. Even now I could feel him mighty in the rocks and mighty in the clouds. Suddenly a bald eagle swooped down into the bowl and circled me without flapping, as if this was the very event I had long searched the trail for. I was flooded with feelings of fatherly love. But enough reflection!

I mounted CJ and flew like the wind, arriving home in impossible time. When I say *impossible*, I mean it. It was not possible to make the first half of the climb, let alone my minutes of prayer and reflection and the visitation from the eagle then the descent, with such speed. Somehow my prayers had altered time, and not for the first time.

Back at the ranch, I dismounted and did what one is never supposed to do: I put my CJ away without brushing him down. He was covered in sweat. Imagine being covered in fur then covered in sweat. You just can't be brushed down after that. It's like what I imagine being waterboarded is like to a human.

That's when I was told to call my brother by my usually frank secretary, who could not look me in the eye.

I knew Dad was dead. The search for the trail to the peak made sense. The bowl on the other side made sense. It was the theater New Mexico had chosen to have that eagle either reflect or possess the spirit of my father and bid me farewell.

The next day I read the cold type of the *Los Angeles Times* account of my father's life with every possible reaction. It was too matter-of-fact. It was not matter-of-fact at all. The facts were too terse. The facts were inaccurate. The facts didn't matter. My father was a dreamer. He never stopped his wistful and wishful dreaming of new ideas about some business or activity. He was full of dichotomies, a rhythm I inherited. He'd secretly donated all of the land for Berkeley Hall's new Mulholland campus, over one hundred acres with hilltop views. Yet, he would not get us two cans of tennis balls when they got to be a dollar a ball. (You can't play tennis with three balls and establish a rhythm.) He never once in his life turned on a radio or played a record. He did sing songs from long ago when the only light at night was the glow of a campfire or a kerosene lamp. My father didn't see a fence until he was nine. Now he was finally free.

I silently saluted him and bade him farewell. I knew that, along with my mother, he had formed my heart. He and she had indoctrinated me into the faith of Christian Science, without which I would be lost. But without *him*, would I be lost? Or without him, would I, as a fatherless son, finally find myself? Or would it grieve me because, for all that was good and bad about my pioneering father, I loved him? Yes, I loved him. I love him still.

FLAGSHIP BUSHMAN

Man see flagship
Man see hewn-away
Petroglyphs on planets
Near enough to touch
Man from the first man
Harmony in beautiful brutal nature
Symphony of tones together
System
See true color
Survival of the mischief
That made the music man's example
Echo of bird, wind and wail
Of unity within the veld
Tranquility the decomposing
Promise of life as
Man see seasons man see flagship day
Stay close to the permanent ambition
Do not go away

—Botswana, 1981

The Kudu

Africa is my escape, Africa is my home, Africa is the home of the human race, Africa is where fear meets faith and faith is found in the sheer beauty of God's august creations. I was in southern Africa, near the border of Botswana, with my bosom buddy Bowen Boshier, African-born under a baobab tree to an Englishman who was among the continent's greatest adventurers. Bowen's dad was consumed by a burning love for Africa that brought him to the continent's hardest, deepest, and most tender territory. Bowen himself is a brilliant artist whose disarmingly simple sketches capture the souls of wild animals, birds, bushes, and trees. His mother's maiden name was van Gogh. That's right—a direct relation to the great one. Bowen combines Hemingway and Kerouac. His mind is startlingly alert, rich and delirious with life lessons. In Africa, Bowen is my man.

We were driving through the jungle in a Land Rover the dusty color of the Kalahari Desert. He took me to a bat cave filled with sleeping bats hanging upside down. They looked like dark fruit, ripened

Bowen Boshier

and ready to be plucked. Bowen brought out his sketchpad and went to work. I watched in wonder.

Then it was back through the bush. The Land Rover made headway, although slowly. Bowen had deflated the tires to half their normal pressure in order to navigate the sandy road. Bowen knew what he was doing. But neither Bowen nor I could react in time to stop a kudu–an enormous antelope whose lethal horns were each three feet long–from crashing into our vehicle. Just as I saw that we were about to be impaled and sent off to African heaven, Bowen swung into action. Forget Johnny Ringo or Doc Holliday. Forget Iceman and the Russian MiGs. This was life-and-death quicksilver maneuvering from a man who realized that the kudu had been compromised. The Land Rover had torn into his side, raising his fury. Seeing the kudu racing down the road, Bowen extracted the foot-long bowie knife from his utility belt and chased after the magnificent beast, leaving me in the Land Rover. Bowen wanted to put the animal out of its misery. Knowing Bowen had a pistol, I shouted, "Why don't you shoot? You'll never catch him!" But catch him he did. The kudu-Bowen battle was ferocious, Bowen finally able to leap on the kudu's back like a calf roper and slash his windpipe. He later told me that he couldn't get to his pistol, and besides, this was the most merciful way to do the job. Our Land Rover had been rendered inoperable. The kudu had kicked in the radiator. Bowen's legs were torn to hell from running through the brambles. In grave despondence, we limped to a local motel. Bowen was devastated. He had killed a creature whom he respected and loved. He applied alcohol to his wounds. He downed a tumbler of whiskey. He had every right to get drunk. As far as I knew, he may have been drunk all day. I wasn't sure. I asked him to get a quote on repairing our Landie, and then went to be alone in my quarters.

So in this moment of confusion when fear was still fresh, what did I do? I did what any actor would do. I called my agent.

"Where the hell have you been, Val? I've been trying to reach you for weeks."

"I've just seen a man kill a kudu with his bare hands. And before that, I spent the morning in a bat cave."

"Say that again, Val."

"I spent the morning in a bat cave."

"That's too weird."

"Why?" I asked.

"They want you to play Batman."

"What?"

"Yeah. F—in' Batman, Val."

"Is it a one-shot or a series?"

"Three. They want you in the next three Batman movies."

"What's the money like?"

"By the third Batman, you'll get ten million."

"Well, I'll have to read the first one."

"Read it? Are you kidding, Val? Just do it."

That's when I started laughing, coughing up Kalahari dust and feeling like I was in a trance.

Was this all really happening? Had I been in a bat cave? Had Bowen slaughtered the kudu? Did Hollywood really want me in the rubber suit?

Yes, yes, yes, and yes.

Batman, but Forever?

I was buzzed about being Batman but hardly for artistic reasons. I had also begun developing a feature film version of *The Saint*, a British spy TV show starring Roger Moore. My idea was to replace Moore in the movie and turn it into a franchise. With two franchises going—*Batman* and *The Saint*—I could start an artists' community, write poetry and plays, and become the wild auteur I saw as my destiny.

The truth is that *Batman* became a trap, and the trap was the suit— the slick, sexy, ridiculous leather-and-rubber slippery contraption that, in theory, transformed Bruce Wayne from man to god. It took an hour to get the thing off and on. That's because Tim Burton's vision for the earlier films had been that the dolphinlike suit be completely seamless. The current director felt obligated to use the same design. The suit was masterful, but once I was in it, I could barely move.

If I dropped something I couldn't pick it up. I could hardly see, could hardly hear, and sure as heckfire couldn't react with any kind of bodily precision. I couldn't really sit and could barely stand. The only way to get my bearings between takes was to lie in a chaise longue. You pushed your feet down and the whole thing magically reclined.

The chair became my friend, my crush, and my only comfort. Oh, how I adored that chaise longue! It was in that wondrous piece of furniture that I experienced an epiphany. I was brought back to high school theater, where, playing old characters, I applied gobs of makeup and was often weighed down by heavy costumes. The result was that I moved like an eighty-year-old. Now the rubber suit was having the same effect. Here I was, supposedly the world's most agile man, who could fly like a bat yet had to struggle to take two steps. In order to answer the call of nature, it took forty-five minutes to undo my suit.

My costars were formidable: Two-Face was played by Tommy Lee Jones, already a friend from the southwest where he also owned a home; the Riddler was played by Jim Carrey, who was the hottest comedian on earth and easy to get along with; and Bruce Wayne's love interest, the sexy psychologist Dr. Chase Meridian, was played by Nicole Kidman. I've always loved Australians—they're frank and fun—and Nicole was perfect in the role. Unfortunately, there was a great deal of unspoken pain during the production. Jim's dad had just died, and one of the first days of shooting he told us a tearful story about how a relative had walked up to him at the funeral with a headshot and asked for his autograph. I was still mourning my dad. We were a sad bunch of superheroes. Everyone's emotions were raw. Our director, Joel Schumacher, brought kindness to spare. He was charming to strangers and family members (and especially gracious with my mother), and for the most part sensitive on set. But everyone has their tough days and there's always super pressure with superhero films as they burn about 100,000 calories a day.

The most fun during *Batman* was watching what seemed like half

As Batman

the Hollywood community bring their kids to see me in costume. As it turned out, one quick glimpse of Batman was enough. I always thought they needed something from the man in the suit. No way. Every single kid transformed into the Bat themselves. I could have been Betty White in there and they wouldn't have minded a bit.

Even my own son would come to be obsessed with Batman. But he couldn't have cared less that I played Batman in a movie. Years later, I tried to watch *Batman Forever* with my family. My daughter, who was maybe five, had come to me while I was deep into my African screenplay and demanded that I prove to her brother that I, their father, was Batman—not him.

"Daddy," she said, "Jack is being such a nuisance and he won't stop saying that he is Batman and not you. Can you *please* prove to him he is wrong?"

"And how am I to do that?" I asked.

"I don't know, show him the movie?"

Since we didn't own a copy I had to purchase one in town. (No streaming back then, kids.) They stayed in the room for about twelve minutes and then quietly walked out. Like a chump, I sat and watched the entire rest of the film.

Kids don't want to play Batman. They want to *be* Batman. And the same with the fans. They don't stay for the glamour. They stay for the truth of a man who struggles with good and evil, who switches from the profane to the sacred and takes it all in stride. The Hamlet who chooses *to be*.

And what about the end product, the film itself?

I mean, it's so bad, it's almost good.

I regret the kitschiness, in a way, because the character himself is one of America's great pop archetypes. Comic heroes resonate on visceral levels. Batman could be a character out of Ovid's *Metamorphoses*. He contains his opposites. He's good, he's bad, he's human, he's a bat, he's a buddy to Robin, he's a lover to gorgeous gals, he's in hiding, he's out in the open, he's vulnerable and he's invulnerable, he's solid and he's flighty. Like so many superheroes, he's able to extend the ordinary into the extraordinary and defy mortality. Born during the Great Depression eighty years ago, Batman has fired the imaginations of countless kids while raking in billions for the comic book and film industries. You gotta hand it to Batman. He's far greater than any actor attempting to play him.

Take the *Heat*

Moviemaking is all about scheduling, logistics, and the mysteries of fate. In the last days of 1994, Warner Bros. changed course. The original plan—to take two years before starting the next *Batman* film—was scrapped. The studio was now insisting that they wanted back-to-back Batman films. Preparation for the follow-up to *Batman Forever*, *Batman and Robin*, was to commence immediately. I just couldn't. That's because I had already committed to doing *The Saint* in London and had been asked to do *Heat*, which was in pre-production, while *Batman Forever* was still shooting. None of this made Joel Schumacher happy or inclined to speak favorably of me to the press. But I had to take the *Heat*.

My agent at the time strongly recommended that I pass.

"Are you kidding?" I asked.

"Val, the pay is less than your per diem for *Batman*."

"But it's Michael Mann directing. And it's Pacino and De Niro. If I do the movie, I'll get to call them Al and Bob for the rest of my life."

"Financially it makes no sense."

But I wasn't thinking finances. I was thinking folklore. Oh, just to collect some deeply nuanced, joyous stories about the *Godfather* films! Just to be able to say "Al and Bob" for the rest of my life!

Director Michael Mann asked how he could repay me, knowing he could never match my rate. I thought about how De Niro and Pacino had been in only one film together in thirty-five years but never shared a scene. And I thought, *Hell, why not be on the poster, sandwiched right between them?* A Hollywood tone poem that would stay with me the rest of my days. Mann agreed. And there I am, pictured below two acting beasts, both of whom were mighty motivators for me to become a beast myself.

Rehearsals began. I drove up on weekends while shooting *Batman*; Bob flew in from Vegas, where he was shooting *Casino*. And Al was shooting *Finding Richard*, his documentary about creating the Shakespeare role he is married to, Richard III. The run-throughs were a little hair-raising for some cast members not used to live ammunition. I was used to it because even before I went to THE Juilliard School I had practiced with the weapons used in westerns, most commonly the Colt .45 six-shooter, meaning it held six bullets; the Winchester 73, the most powerful rifle that was used in securing the West for the white man; and of course the shotgun. My grandfather no doubt owned all three of these staples of the Wild West, and I practiced just like the western heroes of the silver screen before me—practiced quick-drawing, marksmanship, and, most important of all, gun safety on my father's ranches, which, as he increased their sizes decade by decade, seemed a proper use of the rapidly developing land around Chatsworth, with McDonald's on its way toward paving away all trace of natural grace and supplanting the valley with neon and automation and "progress."

I am sorry for the digression, but I want you to understand how it wasn't magic when I was shown how to use the AR-15 by our secret assault team members amassed from around the world by Michael Mann. I was immediately assigned to assisting the actors who knew nothing or very little about the weapons and how to safely break them down and build them back after each heavy practice session, as I had taught myself for years. This was the way I had come to be, by my grandfather and his father before him, making sure his weapons were safe from the gunk that builds up inside a grease-hungry weapon, a weapon used by my grandfathers' era only to survive and defend. There was no money in our family by this time to shoot for marksman ribbons at county fairs. No, all that was left of the Kilmer legacy was that I was such a fast shooter and reloader of the weapon of choice of the last men living out an impossible dream of a valid Wild West.

I have heard, from more than one person, over at Pensacola's naval training camp they show the shootout scene in *Heat*, the sequence of

With actor Tom Sizemore in *Heat*

me firing and reloading this terrifying weapon—so fast it's faster than they require, or can expect their greatest frontline warriors to reload. Their instructors humiliate their best and brightest with such taunts as, "You children, you pawn scum, you motherless excuses of war weapons"—I'm pretty sure the armed services have altered their style of education to something more sophisticated than humiliating and berating our fine military cadets, I'm just sayin' what I heard—"you gonna let some *Top Gun* beach bum actor livin' la vida loca in Hollywood beat you at reloading your own weapon?" That scene was presented without a cut, Michael Mann later told me, because they were all so proud of this dedicated killer elite he had created the image of.

Michael is a ridiculously impassioned man. I love ridiculous passion. One time for research he had Robert De Niro, Tom Sizemore, and me case a bank in bulletproof vests and fake weapons, and the only employee he told was the manager. This I still find hard to believe because of the inherent danger. What if someone who had a concealed weapons permit saw Bob's fake pistol sticking out the back of his Armani? Whoa boy, can you imagine the headaches if not the actual life-threatening drama? This kind of research is like a dream. It must be a dream. Michael never wants to sleep. He wakes in the middle of the night with cinematic visions. He's all tenacity and grit, no sheepishness, no half-baked musings. Michael was methodical to the point of, well, infinity. We would still be shooting *Heat* if they had let him. We shot two entire versions of the famous bank robbery scene, the first with stand-ins. That allowed us to study the whole arc of the scene before we enacted it. I thought that the stand-in version was better than the real take. Michael didn't care. Like a great actor, Michael was always in the moment. He can be guilty of overthinking but always returns to raw instinct as a guide. I loved working with him, even when he insisted that I visit Folsom State Prison, where my character had once been incarcerated. That made little sense, since by then the movie was half-shot and I had already formed my character. But Michael wouldn't back off. So me and his secret weapon, the artist and photographer Gusmano Cesaretti—who has been with Michael since his *Miami Vice* days—flew up to Folsom, where the air was thick with despair. It was the heaviest vibe I'd ever felt—heavy with angst—convincing me that my crazy director wasn't so crazy after all. The visit gave me an edge that I could lend to those final scenes I shot. Besides, no one pays the actor to do research, ever. Getting paid to do research after the film has started? That's just beautiful. I love you, Michael. Always have, always will.

One final Michael Mann story that people in Hollywood have admiringly passed around for years:

He was directing *The Last of the Mohicans* and shooting through the night. Michael was in full manic mode, ready to shout "Action!" for the next scene, when he started panting and whisper-yelling, *"This light. Who hung this light? This isn't right. Get me the gaffer. I'm firing his ass. Who hung this crazy light?"*

A producer gently walked over and whispered, "Michael, it's the sun."

Of course the glory in doing *Heat* was the master class put on by Bob and Al. After watching them at close range, I'd sum it up like this:

Al is Jackson Pollock. He throws it all out there. It lands where it lands. There's no holding back. Bob is Vermeer. Painstakingly, he lays one brick after another until the construction is solid as a rock. Both Bob and Al get to the same place—they embody the characters they play—but they take radically different paths to arrive there. Like children at a funeral, Bob, Al, and I giggled our way through the long nights of this dark movie.

Birth & Death

J ack Kilmer came into this world on June 6, 1995.

Glory, hallelujah!

Much like the birth of my daughter, Mercedes, the birth of my son required that Joanne have a walking labor routine. This time it occurred over two days, not three, and there was no horse suffering a colic convulsion. There was, however, the complication of an especially difficult breech birth—feetfirst and upside down—that seemed to require a caesarean.

We were hard at work reassuring Joanne that a caesarean was a totally fine, normal option and clean operation. The doctor who arrived had answered a 911 call and run to the hospital straight from the gym in neon-pink shorts. She looked sixteen. But she informed us she'd delivered over five hundred babies and that Jack had actually now turned around, poised to be born without any assistance. The moment had arrived, and our doctor looked at us wide-eyed. Joanne screamed, "What do I do now?" And we all screamed back, "Push!"

The nurse breathlessly whispered, "It's a miracle," as he was born, as if we were in a Frank Capra melodrama.

Oh, Jack. You didn't want to leave the sanctity of that warm eternity, but once you realized your destiny, you flew.

Joanne never looked more gorgeous. What is more incredible than a woman being all she can be? That's it for me.

Carly Simon used to call James Taylor her husband long after they divorced. I asked her why. She replied sweetly, "Val, once you have children, you never really separate. It's just a different kind of marriage. Either a good marriage or a bad one. James and I will always be married through our children. There's nothing else at the end of the day." I never did forget it. I wish I had the maturity to live by it.

The birth of a precious child coincided with the unraveling of our union. I'm not sure *blame* is a helpful term. *Blame* implies judgment, of myself and Joanne, and I'm inclined to avoid both. I mentioned before how when we first married I was convinced that the survival of our relationship depended upon our being together during every movie each of us made. When that plan withered, so did our rapport. I felt shut out of my parental role. I remember Joanne suggesting I take down some artwork by my baby brother, Wesley. I should have shut up and done what she asked. It was too much for her to cope with every day, walking past his dark archive of genius, a strange challenge or impossible competition. But rather than try to empathize, I took it as rejection. I felt that one day, along with Wesley's drawings, I'd be asked to leave as well.

Surely Joanne has many reasons we couldn't make a go of it. Given her intelligence and sensitivity, I'm certain those reasons have merit. I am not an easy man. She is not an easy woman. Artists are rarely easy. Actors are never easy. Something between us had died long ago.

I learned about her decision to divorce while watching television in Ireland visiting Brando to discuss a movie we would soon start shooting—our first together. It was broadcast on CNN as a hard news story. Such was my fame at the time after the success of *Batman Forever*. I could have wished for a gentler mode to convey the message, but Joanne had made her decision and had moved to Los Angeles without telling me. I had made mine as well. I was off to Australia to make *The Island of Dr. Moreau*.

The Island Is Dr. Moreau

S hot in the stifling humidity of a lush Australian rain forest, *The Island of Dr. Moreau* was as sublime as it was ridiculous. The sublimity had everything to do with Marlon. Emotionally, I was a wreck. The implosion of my nuclear family left me more vulnerable than I had been at any time in my life. Marlon sensed that and became my dad. He listened to me for hours on end. He comforted me, less with words than his understanding heart. He didn't pry, he didn't look for reasons, he steered me away from regret. Like a guardian angel, he nursed me back to emotional health.

Our bond had been built since his son Christian shot to death the boyfriend of Marlon's daughter Cheyenne. Marlon and his team of lawyers convinced Christian to plead guilty and cut a deal with the DA. Such a turn of events would have made the sanest man mad, but Marlon handled it. During that horrific period, we took a couple of long rides around the city where he weighed the consequences of a trial versus a plea. He was there for his family and I tried to be there for him.

That had happened some five years earlier. Since then, Marlon had done all he could to protect his children. He had struggled courageously and found his way back to his profession. He saw Moreau as a character he could play with his own brand of dark, idiosyncratic humor. "Absurdity," he said to me, "will set us free. At least for a few months."

In those initial days, Marlon was in an expansive mood. He was looking forward to the film. *The Island of Dr. Moreau* is a science fiction novel written by H. G. Wells in 1896, a masterpiece of the genre. This was its third adaptation as a major motion picture with a huge budget. Richard Stanley, who had dreamed up the project and written the screenplay, was also directing. But among a thousand other moving pieces on that set, he was replaced just a few days into production by the legendary John Frankenheimer, who had gained major Hollywood clout for films like *Birdman of Alcatraz* and *The Manchurian Candidate*. Bruce Willis was originally the costar but dropped out when his wife, Demi Moore, filed for divorce. Divorce was in the air.

As Dr. Moreau, Marlon played an insane Nobel-laureate scientist who crossbreeds humans with animals that he manipulates with a remote control. I stumble on his island and become his unwilling assistant. Early on, I saw a little-person actor who I thought might serve as my assistant. Marlon liked the idea—another lark—and decided to adapt it for his character. I lost my mini-me to Marlon but didn't mind. Marlon used his collaborator to great dramatic effect.

Marlon was covered in white cake makeup, reminding me of how he had looked when we first met. On his head he wore an enormous bowl which he had dumped the fruit out of in his trailer. He put in false teeth and turned to me, unable to hold his laughter, and shouted with arms out and wild jazz hands, à la Jimmy Durante, "Oh Val, we're

Marlon Brando on the set of *The Island of Dr. Moreau*

going all the way with this one." I fell on the floor and laughed till my sides hurt. What else are you going to do with a script that really doesn't work? Here we were, two shattered but courageous costars, and a third, an actor I had lobbied heavily for, David Thewlis, whose acting had made Mike Leigh's *Naked* an independent classic.

On our first day, Marlon asked me to his trailer and instructed me to assemble everyone in the film. He wanted to meet them. It didn't take me too long to assemble what I assumed was "everyone," which I took to mean the stars, cinematographer, first assistant director, and other crew who most interacts with the talent. When these fifteen or so people were assembled outside his trailer as instructed, he peeked out through the venetian blinds and mumbled, "What the f—, Val? I said 'everyone.' There are only a dozen people out there."

"Sorry," I said. "I thought you meant just the people important to you in the film."

He looked at me with one of those tough guy looks he invented that can wither metal.

"Everyone's important to me," he said.

So I went out and apologized and redirected the crew to please assemble everyone, from the drivers to the cooks to the wardrobe to the grips and gaffers to the electrical and lighting and camera departments–the entire cast and crew, a couple hundred people. They happily, gleefully lined up to meet the maestro. Everyone wanted to meet Marlon, and Marlon knew it, and the most efficient way to do that wasn't to interrupt the flow of filming–people shuffling up to him and coyly asking for an autograph. No, meet 'em all and get the lay of the land.

When all that was done, we settled into the first scene we were to shoot, which was Marlon's first scene in the film. Which had lots of writing problems. Effortlessly, Marlon solved each and every one of them like the genius he is. He sang a song in Yiddish then another ditty in German and spoke in about seven different languages–French, Spanish, Italian, and a perfect English aristocrat dialect, which is often attempted and rarely successful. He took the curse off my character's clunky exposition, and made the whole introduction to his character nothing short of the feeling of watching a three-ring circus performed and announced by only one man. Marlon Brando was a genius at improv, and it was one of the greatest virtuoso live acting performances I have ever witnessed.

But I told you when we started that this is a blues tone poem so get ready for some serious heartache.

All this was our rehearsal, and I had begged our new director to film it. I'd spent enough time with Marlon to know he doesn't repeat himself, and he's easily bored or distracted. And it's Marlon Brando for god's sake. And film is the cheapest commodity on a set. Roll it, man, 'cause it's never going to be the same twice.

John Frankenheimer didn't roll it.

After Marlon had finished, the applause from the crew was deafening. I looked at John. He, too, was clapping, though, it seemed to me, cursorily. I was a little concerned about that, and about Marlon's health because he had after all just met about two hundred people, and although we were in the shade it was still summer in Australia in a rain forest where the humidity might as well have been one hundred percent. Sweat was pouring off him. I wanted to get him inside some air-conditioning. I was delighted to hear John was thinking the same, as he invited Marlon and me to join him in his trailer. At least, I thought that's what he said. Then I realized he invited us to meet in Marlon's own trailer.

This wasn't right. Trailers on movie sets are like Switzerland. Really, they're private property—space on loan from a studio. If an actor doesn't want to come out of their trailer, no one can make them short of threatening a lawyer or withholding their paycheck.

Once Marlon and I were in his trailer, he instructed me to let John in. "The Weisenheimer," Marlon used to call him in the sanctity of his trailer, and so we all sat in the suddenly heavy air John brought in with him. Damn, what could make this guy so unhappy after having witnessed what we just had? It would have been like if you were a baseball fan and were able to see Babe Ruth knock one out of the park with the bases loaded in the bottom of the ninth in the last game of the World Series. I ain't lyin', Marlon was coming in at around four hundred eighty pounds, but he floated around that set like he was Baryshnikov onstage at the height of his powers.

As we sat, John put both his index fingers up his massive nose for some reason, which immediately captured Marlon's attention, and he looked at me as if we were about to wrestle a leopard, thrilling but oh so dangerous. I could tell Marlon would never forget this moment, this gesture being something he had never seen before. But he had to have known it was really bad news we were about to hear. Marlon had X-ray vision and knew the human heart so well you might as well say he was clairvoyant. Perhaps he was. I only saw him be wrong about someone's motives or objectives once or twice in my whole life. He just never missed.

Could we make it through this meeting without bursting into laughter and destroying this fragile man's ego? What was he doing with two index fingers up his nose, the rest of them folded in clear prayerful supplication? Neither of us had ever seen this before. John spoke, index fingers still safely shoved up into their resting place:

"Marlon, I can't improv the movie."

I wasted no time. "My God," I said to John, "do you own an island? Marlon does, just like his character. Do you speak eight languages? Marlon does, just like his character. Are you crazy? Marlon is, just like his character. Are you a genius? 'Cause Marlon Brando is. Just like his character. Why don't we listen to him and do whatever he says? The script just doesn't work well enough as an acting experience and never did, and there's nothing we can do about that except let the genius loose, man."

Marlon surprised me with his cool. He simply leaned back and said, "I understand, John. No worries, mate."

That night Marlon said to me, "It's a job now, Val. A lark. We'll get through it." I was as sad as I've ever been on a set.

Marlon was always upbeat on set. But at night, he mourned his life's private tragedies in silence. Sometimes he invited me to sit beside him. He'd ask me to read him a poem. It might be Yeats or Walt Whitman or a Shakespeare sonnet. It didn't matter. He just wanted to hear the sound of beautiful language. Sometimes he would weep, but never for long. Eventually, he'd ask me to tell the director that he was ready. Courageously, he completed the film.

John Frankenheimer went on to blame me publicly for ruining the movie. I always thought it an odd thing to try to do, blame me for his failure to make an entertaining film, because my character dies halfway through, and the last half of the film sucks as bad as the first. So how do you work that out? I don't blame John for its failure, but he also could have been its savior.

John, who has long since passed, wasn't a bad guy. But he hurt me and he hurt Marlon. Poor John. Poor Marlon. Poor Richard Stanley, the first director who was fired and went feral and lived in the bush with the hippie stoner expats and came to the set in costume as a pigman or a dogman or a catwoman. Sometimes, to blow my mind, he would scream out my name from a sea of hundreds of extras covered in makeup and giant wigs and costumes with antlers and tails and hoofs and claws. I would say to newcomers on our madhouse set, "This isn't *The Island of Dr. Moreau*. The island *is* Dr. Moreau." If you are ever having a really screwed-up day and need to come down right away, tune into the film, and that'll sober you right up.

For obvious reasons, I have never been able to watch the movie. But I also have not been able to forget how deeply I loved Marlon. Years later, a mutual friend of ours called him lazy. I explained that Marlon was not lazy. He was spacey. He was different. He stayed up all night reading, writing, scribbling philosophical and metaphysical thoughts. If, then, I showed up at his house the next afternoon and he fell asleep on the couch right there in front of me, I understood why. His was a wandering, nonlinear spirit. His talent assumed forms I could not always grasp, but his friendship never faltered. He's what I called *STG*—short-term genius. He couldn't plan a lunch for the day after tomorrow, but right there in the moment he may have been the most insightful man of our time.

Crocodiles & Ecstasy

The day we wrapped *The Island of Dr. Moreau*, I flew to Africa for another large-scale production, *The Ghost and the Darkness*, with Michael Douglas as my costar. During the shoot, my closest companion was Cindy Crawford.

My divorce from Joanne led me to Cindy, whom I had known for a while but left alone due to the outside chance that my marriage might be salvageable. When TV told me otherwise, I took up that pursuit without hesitation.

The divorce was brutal. I made the epic mistake of moving the legal procedure from California to New Mexico, so that the children didn't have to be dragged into the mess, as they often are with high-profile divorces. I thought we would have a better chance of a quiet divorce in our home state. Besides, it's where we all lived, though Joanne had just moved to LA to start a new life without me. It was a costly decision. The divorce laws in the Land of Enchantment are less than enchanting; they calculate back earnings in a way that left me pillaged and penniless. In California, the estate is split the day of the separation.

The Pecos River Ranch, with the house in the middle distance

In New Mexico, money earned is calculated as equal until the divorce is finalized, so it's in the lawyers' best interest to have it take as long as possible. The suit dragged on for almost five years, through several teams of lawyers. I kept trying to explain to Joanne that all we were doing was robbing our children of any annuity they might gain from the fortune we were giving the lawyers instead. All I ever wanted was

for Love to reign in our house. I prayed for humility and forgiveness every day for years and years and years.

I had expanded my landholdings in New Mexico from sixteen hundred to six thousand acres, probably the most dazzling six thousand acres in the whole state because of our eleven springs and six miles of the Pecos River and being surrounded on three sides by a national forest. My compound included buildings to hold theaters and workshops. The main house was at once enormous, intimate, and rustic. It was half log cabin, half adobe. The loss of my material world was happening at the same time that I could still demand big salaries. Money was flying in and out. I was dizzy with all the motion.

My marriage was dead but my courtship of Cindy Crawford was alive. We had met at a couple of parties. We flirted. We danced. We joked. We exchanged numbers. Rather than wax rhapsodic, let me present a bullet-point summary of her beguiling nature:

- Cindy is America.
- Cindy is a happy person who loves her family deeply.
- She's an original who re-created her industry, which was at times cruel and perverse, and she did it with grace and without finger-pointing.
- She is a natural athlete and loves glorious things that a man just can't get enough of.
- She loves to cook, and still one of my favorite meals of my entire life is a simple salmon dish that, after our African sojourn, she prepared at her Malibu beach house.

There are at least fifty more bullet points, and I've yet to mention the two that moved me most. One is she's completely honest. How many people can you say that about? The second is related to the first: she's ingenious at making contact, in every single sense. The song, I believe, is called "Body and Soul." You can hear it sung by Sarah Vaughan or played by Stan Getz, but it's Cindy's song. We exchanged crushes. We may have even begun falling in love. But that love wouldn't be confirmed until our time in Africa.

I wanted to show her Africa's majesty. I prepared a surprise dinner by a river that meandered through the rhino preserve where I was filming. I asked some of my closest African friends to help me hours before with a gorgeous bohemian blanket, caviar I had flown in, and fresh local fish prepared by the finest chef in town. I set up Moroccan pillows and selected moody music and asked the heavens for a meteor shower.

I remember being literally dizzy from so many things being right about that night. I never thought of it this way until this moment, but it was our honeymoon. So there we were, completely lost in our love, and if there's one thing Africa is when you really need her to be, she's romantic. Just at the right moment, probably after a divine dessert, the sky rained down stars, falling and shooting up and across, and then blackness and peace. "Peace like a river," as Paul Simon would sing.

So there we were, like some king and queen from a fairy tale, just whispering, "I love you," back and forth, with tears rolling down. And then, in the deafening silence, we heard *kerplunk!* from the river. *Do I tell her it's a crocodile and ruin the moment? No. Here we are in the middle of a perfect night, a perfect life. Are we going to be eaten now? We could have just as easily been eaten earlier, taking a bath. No. But, maybe. But, if we are? Okay.*

Oh God, I loved Cindy and just kept loving her. I thought I could have died from her love, not because it was difficult but because its delight was simply too much to bear. I would die of happiness. I would die of gratitude. I would die if Cindy couldn't accompany me to Moscow, where, after all the lion-killing drama that comprised *The Ghost and the Darkness* was spent, I was due to shoot *The Saint*. I hoped to bring my saint with me.

The Sinner Is the Saint

My bid for an ever-blooming franchise fruit was basically what you might call a Tom and Jerry movie. I put James Bond, Ethan Hunt, Jason Bourne, Jack Ryan, and the rest in this category. The cat tries to catch the uncatchable mouse. All else is window dressing. *The Saint* had lots of window dressing. It was great fun and in some ways opened up the window for the *Mission: Impossible* franchise nailed by Tom Cruise with impassioned athleticism. In *The Saint*, I spoke in a variety of accents, wore a variety of disguises, pulled off a variety of stunts—not as well, I might add, as Cruise or Damon, but I gave it my all.

I must make a public apology to the writer, Wesley Strick, whose characters I refashioned from start to finish. The script was great, but I knew we had the opportunity to do something special with the main character, to be unique. And that always makes people nervous. But I explained to the executives the studio sent out to meet with me and discuss the project that the audience doesn't care about the studio. They don't care about safe choices and good investments. They care about stories, and they want to be moved, to be stirred, to be lifted out of their seats. Impassioned and with every fiber of my being, I pitched my fully fleshed idea, and they went for it.

David Brown, the classiest of all the producers that I had ever worked for—his films include *The Sting* and *Jaws*—upon my initial arrival at Heathrow, was there to greet me holding an umbrella and wearing a three-piece suit, overcoat, and hat. After a grand hug, his first words were, "My star."

I almost wept.

I asked him, "Why are you here? Is Helen on my flight? I didn't see her." (His wife was Helen Gurley Brown, editor in chief of *Cosmopolitan*, who loved me doubly because of Cindy.)

"No, my dear boy, I am here to pick you up and welcome you to London."

I hugged him again. It wasn't fashionable yet to hug men. But I hugged him as though he had just saved my child's life. You don't know what it's like to be respected like that on a film. As crucial as actors are to a project, it just doesn't happen.

During the shoot, there was a coup among the producers that resulted in David Brown's removal, an unfortunate and mistaken move in my opinion. Nonetheless, the film was completed and earned its place, not as the ongoing franchise I had imagined, but as a lively piece of entertainment that had my quixotic character on the run.

Because Cindy was by my side, we had to sneak around a lot, which puts a strain on a girl who has worked her whole life to become a household name. The day after the movie wrapped, she and I began traveling the world. We fell so deeply in love that we started color-blocking the interiors of our imaginary ranch. The living room was rust. The kitchen was coral. The ranch turned out to be real. We were really in New Mexico and I was really living a life outside Hollywood. I credit Cindy with my rebirth after the divorce from Joanne. She was

With Cindy Crawford in Moscow, 1996

always trying hard to make it work–her career and our relationship–always sensitive to my vulnerabilities. And yet always floating a few inches above the ground. Why, then, didn't we last?

Well, I suppose you could say we had a cat-and-mouse thing of our own. Right when I was about to catch her, for a long weekend by the beach or a month in the mountains, she'd disappear. Right when I was walking across the room to hug her, she was leaving to get on a plane. I could hardly blame her. I imagined she spent much of her life fending off the advances of men and, as a result, acquired this defense mechanism that was in equal parts ingenious and infuriating. It was a spiritual bubble, a kind of impermeable membrane, that prevented anyone or anything from disturbing her sense of inner peace, accomplishment, poise, and process.

She scheduled herself down to the quarter hour. She would say, "Okay, Brazil on Monday. France on Wednesday. And then I'll spend the weekend with you." Even then I'd think, *When are you going to just relax and decompress?* She'd fly to spend the weekend with me, and in the car, before she even came inside, her agent would call. She was the world's most in-demand supermodel, and yet she felt a hunger to keep building and growing.

It's a heartbreaker. Cindy was always one step away. We were together for a nearly a year. We didn't have a fight when it was over. It was a conversation about choices.

"When's the last time you took a break?" I asked. I meant it rhetorically, but she stopped to think and, like a comic book hero, placed her hand to her chin. She considered the question in earnest. After several seconds of silence she admitted that she couldn't remember.

I have tried many times to make sense out of my actions and even after all these years, sometimes it just gets too hard to contemplate.

I am glad she is happy. I wish her well.

More, More, More

Years later, I was rescued from an icy inferno of solitude by an-other angel. Perhaps the most soulful and serious of them all. Angelina. When people ask me what Angelina Jolie is like, I always say she's like other women and other superstars, but just *more*. More gorgeous. More wise. More tragic. More magic. More grounded. Is it worth it? Worth knowing people who require weeks of effort to un-derstand even a little? Yes. These paradigms of power and prowess are the women who have inspired men throughout history to fight battles, build nations, and leave their lives and wives behind. I melt at the sight of girls like these. Not because I am masochistic, but because I am a slave to Love. I am a hopeless romantic.

I haven't had a girlfriend in twenty years. My editor—who is not as averse to Googling as I am—says fifteen. But time isn't real anyway, so what's the difference? Time is a dimension that is in constant flux, in-fluenced by gravity, and perhaps a timekeeper. The truth is I am lonely part of every day. We all know how it goes.

Help, I need somebody.

Help, not just anybody.

We sing along with impossible yearning and tap our toes to the beat. No matter what we possess, most of us want more, more, more. Is this the survival instinct and essence of the human being? Or is it just capitalism?

We dream. We desire. We adapt. We play.

Angie didn't remember when I stopped her on the street when she had just wrapped *Gia* and a Rolling Stones music video. I saw her so far down the street that I had enough time to catch my breath and calm down and then work myself back up again and act completely the fool. I told her what she'd heard her whole life. She acted like no one had ever told her she was one of the most striking women in the world. I asked if she was an actress, blah blah blah. I wanted to wash the filthy New York sidewalk for however many miles she cared to cover that crisp autumn day. Years later, when Oliver Stone asked us to play husband and wife (not just husband and wife, but king and queen warring over the very soul of their only son, the future ruler of the entire civilized world), I couldn't help but laugh at the irony. We developed a friendship. I was around when Angie's mom was losing her battle with cancer. They were living in her mom's favorite hotel. Or maybe it was Angie's. I happened to be staying there myself. It was meaningful and mortal and effortless and exquisite.

The film was *Alexander*. I told Oliver I'd only do it if the king and queen could have flashbacks to falling hard for each other and storming the castle with passion, before turning against each other. I was half kidding. He didn't pick up on the humor. "What?" I tried to clarify. Finally I just sighed. "Oh, never mind. I just dig her, Oliver. It would be nice if we had some flashbacks when they were in love and happy together."

With Angelina Jolie at the UK premiere of *Alexander*

Oliver was on a mission to realize his twenty-five-year dream of bringing Alexander to the screen and wasn't in the mood for clowning.

"Get a room, Val. This film isn't about you. It could have been, but I guess you weren't ready."

Ah, there was the old salt-in-the-wound Oliver I'd come to know and love. He was talking about the time right before we'd wrapped *The Doors*, and he was encouraging, but more like demanding, I read all the books I could on Alexander the Great. But I didn't really have a firm grasp on what he wanted to do with it all. It's like saying you're going to do the story of Genghis Khan. *Okay, good luck with that. You're going to film with real armies and cross the Bering Strait? Sure. Gimme a call when you get the money.*

Nevertheless, I couldn't wait to rehearse. I couldn't wait to kiss Angie, buy her a Gulfstream jet, and have *V+J* painted in rainbow glory on the tail. She had recently adopted her first child, Maddox, and the paparazzi were obsessed with this postmodern Madonna, the perfect picture of unapproachable stardom and impossibly chic maternal instinct.

I believe in the power of beauty and the art of Love itself. Now consider, as I must, the reality that the similarities between father and son will be striking to any discerning reader of this book. I like to say I played out my affairs in three acts.

Act I was that I wouldn't reveal myself because I was investigating whether I wanted to marry a girl or not. Then, after we fought and determined we were utterly wrong for each other, I could say, "You don't know me at all." True. But I also hadn't even tried to let her in.

Act II was about trying before I was ready. I married Joanne, ready for the bliss of everlasting companionship but secretly hoping it would heal me and fill in my black holes. Of course only God can fill those holes, a fact that we humans often ignore. So the great depression of our marriage came when we realized that we couldn't fix each other.

Act III incorporates my more recent romantic history. You'll soon see that I worked feverishly at sustaining relationships with two remarkable women. That sustenance was based on being open, grounded, and self-loving, and allowing someone to complement rather than complete me. It takes a wild amount of self-growth and evolution to keep a romance alive. With Cindy, I tried and failed.

In the aftermath of that relationship, I sought peace of mind by reading, reading, reading. Books have always sustained me, especially when the blues blow through like a hurricane. At this point, I rediscovered not only a book but an author I had loved since childhood. On some level, the author's central subject was childhood itself. His genius was in relocating the humor and joy of long-forgotten childhoods. Humor and joy were just what the doctor ordered.

Never the Twain Shall Meet

O ver sixty years ago, well-known Mark Twain scholar Leslie Fiedler wrote an interesting essay about *Huckleberry Finn* in which he argued that the bonding between Huck and Jim involved more than a mischievous white boy escaping civilization in the company of a runaway slave. The article, called "Come Back to the Raft Ag'in, Huck Honey," quotes Jim calling out to Huck. Fiedler points to a bond of luminous Love that defines their relationship. The critic maintains that, beyond the twists and turns of the story, Twain's real subject is more than the exploration of forbidden male-to-male (and white-to-black) Love; Twain is exploring the nature of Love itself. Fiedler saw Twain as I saw Twain: as a religious writer.

At the start of the twenty-first century, I felt myself drawn to Twain in a way I hadn't experienced since childhood. Head-on, he addressed the major issues that haunted America then and haunt it now: the hypocrisy of polite society, the pernicious evil of racism, the essential artistic urge to rail against conformity and find unfettered expression in biting wit and outrageous drama. Huck and Jim are two of the great characters in the history of our literature because of their improbable but absolute need for one another. Twain saw the humanity in the miscreant boy and the desperate slave. He turned hopeless tragedy into hilarious comedy without trivializing the tragedy or compromising the comedy.

The genius of this literary enterprise floored me and had me reading Twain—all of Twain—night and day. Like his books, he was both a comic and a tragic figure. He was the most famous American of his time. He earned and lost fortunes. Fiedler is right to see Twain as primarily "a poet, the possessor of deep and special mythopoetic powers whose childhood was contemporaneous with a nation's." Twain understood the troubled souls of this nation's citizens with the acuity of a devilish saint. He was a lonely leader of a tribe looking for hope. In that regard, he reminds me of Moses.

Oddly enough, I've played Moses three times. The first was in *The Prince of Egypt*, a sleeper Disney hit with a massive all-star cast that included Michelle Pfeiffer and Ralph Fiennes, with music by Hans Zimmer and Stephen Schwartz, sung by Whitney Houston and Mariah Carey. Though making the movie was a solitary experience—me alone in a sound booth—the final product was charming and beloved family fare.

My second Moses was in *The Ten Commandments*, a mortifying-at-best live musical at the Kodak Theatre with a very young Adam Lambert and a bunch of other Broadway kids too talented for the material. The saving grace was that the ridiculous mishaps onstage served to entertain me, bloopers in my mind for many lifetimes. Columns rose and fell. Lines were forgotten. Without realizing it, we were Monty Python and the Holy Fail.

My third and final Man of the Mountain moment was an audio recording for a hip-hop gospel musical version of the story by composer-lyricist Walter Robinson. It was fascinating, and I was delighted to participate.

I suppose you could say I've played Jesus-like characters as well, Jim Morrison being one, Doc Holliday perhaps as well. It's a trip to play superhuman characters while dealing with the most human things in your off time. Custody. Divorce. A looming recession. A very expensive ranch. A dream life that sometimes mirrors your reality and sometimes dwarfs it. A career in which make-believe is real and everything else is just the rehearsal.

I found it grounding, as many make-believers do, to surround myself with friends and lovers who were *real*. One such female friend was an earthy, unpretentious muse, someone with whom, in my dreams, I could still reconcile. She's a yogi and a healer. Jaycee Garnet Gossett.

Soft Opening

It was 2001. I was forty-one. I had briefly been dating a British woman who was severe, austere, and competitive. But her cool factor was unmatched. In many areas, there was undoubtedly stimulation. Our competition lasted through our entire short, spicy, scary relationship to the final meeting, at which point we agreed to dissolve our relationship in New York and began to quietly argue about where exactly the breakup dinner should take place. I wanted to take her somewhere lovely. I still wanted to impress her. I thought maybe a chef's table at a fine restaurant, where we would be walked through a tasting menu of rarefied delicacies. No. Maybe at the top of a tall building. Or a jazz club. She called all my charming ideas lame. Her notion was to take me to a place in SoHo so chic that the general public knew nothing about it. The restaurant had yet to open. But because she knew the chef, and because tonight he was having an invitation-only super-exclusive soft opening, we could get in. What could I say?

"You win," seemed the right response.

The moment I walked into this soft opening, I saw her. Jaycee

Gossett. I might have been hunched over with self-doubt from this failed fling, but Jaycee had me standing straight. She was the maître d' and she was smiling deep from within as golden curls fell all around her shoulders. She was Titania and Helena and Hermia. She was everything.

We locked eyes, and without saying more than five words, she seated us. I listened as my about-to-be-former girlfriend accused me of being irresponsible, impulsive, and childish. I didn't argue. I just wanted to steal secret glances at Jaycee. Right then and there, I wanted to irresponsibly, impulsively marry her. Of course, I couldn't say anything that night.

The following day I went through the motions of errands. Work prep. Calls. Dry cleaner. As the sun set, I put on a crisp linen shirt and sauntered back to the spot. There she was. Freedom. Peace. Connection. Kahlil Gibran says a soul mate is the guardian of the other person's solitude. Gibran was describing what Jaycee meant to me. I knew it. Soon she knew it. We belonged together.

Jaycee and I embarked on a three-year love affair that lives in my body-mind like nothing else. She was a real-life angel, and she was up for anything, as long as it was good for the soul. She was good for the soul. In my *Inside the Actors Studio* interview, James Lipton asked about my favorite sound. I answered, "Any sound coming from my beloved, Jaycee." Most people watching, especially between California and New York, might have thought I meant Jesus Christ. I'm fine with that interpretation.

Like summer camp, everything with Jaycee was fun and new. Because she wasn't a celebrity, she was free of celebrity baggage. We took tourist boats on the Hudson River and felt like we were in Prague.

Once I took her to a party at the Waldorf Astoria, invited by a friend who was an ambassador to the UN. Well, who should show up but the

With Jaycee Gossett, 1999

president of the United States, Bill Clinton. He beelined straight for us, and like the cliché of an actor that I am, I foolishly thought he wanted to talk to me. He indulged me for a few minutes, asking a few questions and answering mine, and then stuck with Jaycee for the next hour and a half. She remained composed without returning an ounce of Clinton's flirtation. She was honored yet unimpressed.

Through her blood ran the salt of the earth, plus some sea salt and a few little shells. She glistened.

So why did it end? 'Cause I'm a fool.

Oh, you want more detail?

'Cause I'm a big fool.

A big stupid fool.

And beyond that, I'm not sure what to say. It's not an issue of fidelity but one of neglect. I disappeared into my role in *The Salton Sea*, and Danny Parker as a partner left a bit to be desired. He's a lethargic, depressed musician addicted to methamphetamine, who moonlights as an informant for corrupt policemen after his wife is gunned down by masked thieves. *If you can't beat 'em, join 'em* might be the subtext of the film, as Parker spiritually sinks deeper and deeper until his only remaining joy is a partnership with a notorious dealer who lost his nose to meth. Well, you saw how much I sank into the Lizard King, and, though it made for good acting, it ruined my relationship. I let the character of Parker swallow me whole, and I was miserable, desolate, without a single sparkle in my eye. In honor of the project and in honor of art, I let Jaycee slip away. And I had done it so many times before her. But Jaycee was perfect. And I think about her every day.

Declarations of Independence

I t was the dawn of a new millennium. I had just hosted *Saturday Night Live*, which was every bit as ecstatic as I had imagined in my flannel pajamas in Chatsworth. A perfect digestif to finish off the past twenty years of my career.

At this point, meanwhile, Hollywood was high on its own strange energy drink of ego, flash, and cash. In an unflinching attempt to empower directors, actors, and other collaborators to honor the truth and essence of each project, an attempt to breathe Suzukian life into a myriad of Hollywood moments, I had been deemed *difficult* and alienated the head of every major studio. I looked at the industry from the inside out, and from the outside in, and in a conscious and deeply satisfying act of authenticity, I hung up my hat.

In my mind, I retired. I decided that my priorities would undergo a massive cognitive shift. In the words of Thoreau, "Rather than love, than money, than fame, give me truth." I remember Mike Ovitz, one of the founders of CAA, telling me I couldn't leave Los Angeles. I had to stay or, at the very least, get a Los Angeles phone number. If I was going to get off the grid, the players would keep on playing. The game of Monopoly would continue at ever-increasing velocity and I would be there, at the very beginning, waiting for someone to pick me up or get me out of jail.

I weighed the options. To constantly chase the high, or to let my feet touch the earth, let my toes feel the sand. And I thought of New Mexico. And I thought of my own dreams of making art and telling stories. And I vowed to myself that I would bring them to life, or die trying.

Gay as a Pink Hairnet

To fully understand my move to New Mexico and why I bought a ranch and kept on buying acres of land like they were vintage T-shirts, you must understand the state. Remember my first visit as an adult? It was to see a sexy older lady with a wealthy swagger, Jane Smith, who lived with Betty Stewart. Jane had coaxed me there when I was a mere youth. On my drive to Jane's, where as a kid I'd seen real cowboys dismount their horses and tie them off in the middle of the town square, all I saw was strip malls and Dunkin' Donuts. All my childhood memories of real cowboys were gone. Discouraged, I called Jane to voice my disappointment. "Just keep going," she said. "You've left hell. You're in purgatory. Paradise is but a few miles away. Have faith, Dante." I soldiered on, past the tourist shops, into the wilderness. Thirty miles later, I arrived. I was transported to the New Mexico of my dreams. Ruins and remnants from old churches and brothels, wild horses, and a little stone path to her glorious ranch, maintained by herself and Betty. As I walked up, they were engaged in a non-lover's quarrel. Jane listened as her tomboy counterpart croaked, "That Sam

Shepard's a phony. And he can't even ride a horse." I'd later learn that was untrue. And also later learn to love Betty for her irreverence.

In the comfort of their strange yet familiar home, I felt angels all around me. It made no difference that Jane and Betty were bickering; I couldn't have been more comfortable. Just as I put down my bags, another character entered the scene. Gordon Edmunds Miller. He was gorgeous and obviously gay. "We've met before," he whispered.

"No." I shook my head. "I don't think so. I never forget a face."

"Well," he countered, "I'm afraid you have."

Gordon jogged my memory of earlier that year, when, while I was living at Caesars Palace with Cher, there had been a fire that forced us to evacuate. The entire hotel had emptied out.

"You and I," he reminded me, "were standing outside on the Vegas strip half-naked. As vain as I might be, I'll forgive you forgetting."

"No, no," I said. "Now I do remember."

He rewarded me with a hug. Gordo was acerbic, rad, and one of a kind. He soon became one of my dearest friends. We had a holy connection. So was my connection to Sam Shepard, horseman, cowboy, writer, actor, poet, and enthusiastic drinker. Later in my New Mexican life, his enthusiasm was demonstrated when one night he drove to my ranch and couldn't get the gate to open. He'd forgotten the code. Rather than turn around and go home, or think to call me, he rammed through the gate that bore the beautiful brand of my ranch, a logo designed by my dad, and a dream I had been proud to realize for him. Like a real cowboy, instead of apologizing, he eventually did something deeper. He gave me his most precious vintage pair of sterling silver spurs. He correctly understood that they'd be worth more to me than any gate. Tell me that's not a cowboy.

Sam and Gordo were friends, but I suspect that the only cowboy film Gordo ever saw was *Brokeback Mountain*. That was fine with me. I loved the film myself. Gordo was a world-class wit and elegant advocate for the LGBTQ+ community before they found their nomenclature. He lived beyond labels. An enlightened soul, his circle of tight-knit comrades included Jane Fonda and a host of members of the literati. Gordo was as refined as they come, hailing from a hoity-toity California family with recent roots in San Francisco but blue blood from back east. I mean, so blue Gordon's family told him they didn't have to hop on the *Niña*, the *Pinta*, or the *Santa Maria*. When Gordon asked his uncle why, the answer was, "My dear boy, those ships were for those who couldn't afford their own."

Gordo would tell me how every few days his dad wandered into one of the banks he owned to work as a teller, just for the sake of humility. Unlike his dad, Gordo showed no interest in clerical duties. He admonished his experts to play with his money strictly with the aim of making more. I loved the cavalier nature of his buying and selling. A quick fax. A five-word phone call. He executed complex transactions with all the grace of Fred Astaire in *Funny Face*. Gordo's dinners were grand affairs. Like Elliott Templeton in Somerset Maugham's *The Razor's Edge*, Gordo was the perfect balance of polite and

Gordon Miller

outrageous. He chose his guests judiciously but always with an eye for entertainment. Queens were invited to his table along with ranchers, gardeners, dancers, painters, and priests.

I'm afraid I wasn't always the best guest. With certain groups, I can come on a bit strong. The New Mexican art elite found me feral, and I found them vapid. Yet Gordo's innate humanity and extreme sensitivity always brought me back into the fold. He made me feel welcome.

Gordo trained show horses. He himself was an accomplished horseman. Rain or shine, he and I rode for hours. Our only obstruction was a ravenous wild dog scouring the area for scraps in all its diseased bliss. We had some close calls but managed to avoid the deranged beast, galloping off in the nick of time, riding into the sunset as our equestrian guides, covered in joyous sweat, led us home.

Gordo was the first of my friends to surf the initial wave of the World Wide Web. He combed sites for poignant stories and perfect punch lines to share during his sophisticated soirées. At Gordo's, a Michelin-level meal was always awaiting me, not to mention vintage wine and just the right mixture of sages and fools. His poise cracked only when he told jokes at my expense. They usually entailed a fabulously exaggerated story insinuating some queer love triangle between him, myself, and an unknown third party. He built so slowly and powerfully to the climax of the story that it was too heartbreaking (or just not worth it) to correct him. And at the same time, it was annoying to have things hinted that were simply made up. He went so far as to tell a woman who was interested in me that he and I were living together. The truth is that, due to whatever crazy circumstances I happened to be in, I was living in a tent on his expansive property with the ulterior motive of running inside to grab bacon and eggs in the morning. The woman presumed we were sharing a bed.

Gordo couldn't resist a joke in which the straight man turns out not to be straight at all—either that or is portrayed as a buffoon.

One evening I had had enough. I pulled him aside and said, "Gordo, you're a Republican. I'm a Democrat. But I've never ridiculed or even mentioned your politics in public, have I?"

"No, you haven't."

"Well, I feel like there are times when you ridicule my heterosexuality."

"An interesting perspective."

"More hurtful than interesting. I'm straight, and being straight doesn't give you the right to turn me into the punch lines of your jokes."

"I didn't know you see it that way."

"I think you'd see it that way if I made gay jokes and used you as the punch line."

"Don't get all huffy, Val. I'm the first to describe myself as gay as a pink hairnet."

"That's cool, but that's you making light of yourself."

"You can treat me as lightly as you like, Val."

"I'm not looking for a shooting match. I'm just asking you to treat me well."

I could see Gordo was ready with a quick retort. But instead he said nothing. Several seconds ticked by. His battle-ready body language relaxed. He looked at me with softened eyes.

"I hear you, Val," he said. "I really do. And I know you're speaking out of friendship and love."

And so our Love and friendship grew even stronger. From that day forward, Gordo was always my first call during the most meaningful moments of my life. He was always prepared with a worldly line of poetry—Seamus Heaney was a favorite—to honor whatever moment I was in.

Gordo, who died at age fifty-four in 2006, left us all with the hope that true friendship, like Love, can heal the deepest wounds. His close friend the writer Dominick Dunne said in his eulogy, "Gordo treasured his friends and his friends treasured him back. He was a social historian who lived removed from society; the telephone was his connection to a world that he had forsaken. He was hilariously funny. He loved to dish. He was wonderful."

BIG DEAL HAIKU

I told you—
You tell her & you tell everyone
You have what of that
The honey drips off our
California lineage tree
Trillionth of a second
Our world human history
Big deal
Our affair
Big deal
You and me

—Ware, England, 1987

Siren on a Snowboard

New Mexico was every bit as healing as I'd hoped. I'd managed to marshal my financial resources. I had my ranch. I had my career. And then the universe smiled and said, "Meet Daryl Hannah." Daryl was and always will be a spirit ahead of her time. (Neil Young, I always loved you, but I'm afraid I hate you now.) She was kind of the female me, except better. She'd found fame at seventeen and then turned her back on it. She thought, analyzed, and articulated ideas so rapidly that by the time I caught up she was already on to a new cycle of insights. She had been rock royalty since befriending U2 at the start of their careers. The Irish boys recognized her divinity.

She and I were once at the Grammys while U2 was racing at a ferocious clip along the trailers outside the auditorium. They were due onstage. Yet when Bono saw Daryl, he hit the brakes so suddenly that his über-expensive handmade working-class boots screeched like he was in a Laurel and Hardy sketch. (Not to ridicule Bono's boots. It's just jealousy. I'm a boot fanatic myself.) Bono and the band stacked up like dominoes atop one another when they realized it was Daryl.

She let go of my hand and crowd-surfed into their arms. The rock stars turned into teenage superfans, their worship of this woman authentic and pure. I knew that even if they scored a dozen Grammys that night, after the show they'd still be talking about running into Daryl.

I don't want to stop talking about Daryl. I want to remember the morning we awoke in her exquisitely refurbished barn in Telluride. Leaning against a wall was a remarkable piece of art, a long, wide plank of wood. I saw it as a daring piece of avant-garde sculpture. I had to know the name of the sculptor. Daryl laughed and said, "It's just my snowboard." I looked it over again and realized she was right. But who made it? "Jake Burton Carpenter," she said without a hint of pretense. "He invented the modern snowboard. He said he'd never made one for a woman. This was his first. The weight, the strength, the design, the split tail. Isn't it fun?" Of course it was fun. Of course she'd be the first woman for whom Burton would fashion a snowboard. I imagined that the first ladies' tennis racket was made for someone like Daryl, a six-foot-tall Amazonian tower of delicate power, that same kind of woman who inspires men to invent myths, blow up castles, and leave their queens.

The next day Daryl and I hit the slopes. She disappeared so quickly it was like sleight of hand. By the time I caught up, she was surrounded by a group of guys who had either spotted her or chased after her. They all stood on a perch where world-class snowboarders paused to stare at the peasants. I wanted to die. They were legitimate X Games champs and gold medal winners, men who owned mountains and countries. They considered Daryl their equal.

As best as I could detect, Daryl contained no negativity. Even a man she had dumped, the world's most eligible bachelor–John F. Kennedy Jr.–continued cultivating her company. During the Daryl/John-John courtship, the press went wild because Daryl wouldn't say a word about Jackie. The media manufactured a nasty buzz over a supposed rivalry between Daryl and Jackie. Lies. Daryl and Jackie adored one another. They forged an indelible friendship. Daryl was incapable of describing Jackie's last days without weeping. Jackie asked Daryl to come into her bedroom, sit by her side, and listen to her final stories. Far more than speaking, listening is the ultimate act of Love. Daryl also spoke the unvarnished truth. At the Academy Awards, in her golden dress and tinted eyeglasses, her hair dramatically coiffed, she stood apart. On that night of nights, her way of being was so effortless, so absurdly attractive, yet so mocking of the event that claims legitimacy in lifting one artist above another.

"Why burden an actor by suggesting the finest moment of his life is inferior to someone else's?" she asked me. "If I ran the Oscars, I'd re-language the awards. No more absolutes. No more certainties. No more 'best.' Instead, 'A recognition of a defining performance.' 'An acknowledgment of a fearless reenactment.'"

Daryl uttered the most intimate words any woman has ever spoken to me. We had rented a cabin along the Southern California coast. It had been a long day under a punishing sun. My skin was still pulsing. Night had fallen. A cool breeze offered welcome relief. We were both reading scripts. In the distance, an owl's hoot, a nightingale's song, the rustle of leaves. We stayed silent, focused on the pages before us. And then, for no apparent reason, we stopped and faced one another. Eerily, we seemed to be breathing as one. A new harmony. An almost frightening closeness. The owl and songbird, the rustling of leaves, the light of the moon upon Daryl's face. And then her words:

"Val," she whispered, "if we marry and have a boy, can we name him Wesley?"

She touched, opened, and healed my deepest wound, deepest wish, deepest loss. I was moved for days. I floated on a cloud. I knew

At a Lakers game with Daryl Hannah

I would love her with my whole heart forever. That love—invisible, ephemeral, and infinite—has lost none of its strength.

I made mistakes with Daryl. Maybe it was possessiveness. Maybe it was ego. Friends I respect swear by analysis, whether the Freudian or Jungian variety. Friends I respect employ life coaches to help them understand when and why they go off the rails. Millions follow a spiritual path based on those famous twelve steps. I do feel that I am a stepper. By that, I mean that I believe we need to keep on steppin'. I believe in moving forward toward the ultimate goal: unification with a loving God. At the same time I continue to lead my life on the run. Lord knows I've suffered heartache with women. But Daryl was by far the most painful of all.

Suffice it to say, I would have done anything to win her back. God's perfect plan of peace sometimes cannot be understood yet must be followed. I followed a decidedly imperfect path. And yet our connection remains a beacon of hope for the disjointed and lonely.

Hiding from God

I reflect on a thousand and one evenings when, alone, I sought comfort in music. The music might have been John Lennon singing about his "beautiful beautiful beautiful boy." It could have been Van Morrison playing his "healing game" and doing his "moondance." It could have been screaming Led Zep or Janis Joplin demanding that I take another little piece of her heart. It could have been Jack White or the Black Keys or Rage Against the Machine. It could have been a muted Miles whispering "So what?" in his kind-of-blue mode. It could have been cinematic scores that, despite being called cornball by hard-nosed critics, fill my heart with joy—soundtracks to epics like *Lawrence of Arabia* and *Dr. Zhivago*. It could even have been Tony Bennett looking for lost love in San Francisco.

I had foolishly ended things with Jaycee and then foolishly ended things with Daryl. I had overbought land. I was house-poor and alone. I was still fighting for custody of my kids. I could feel the recession looming as well as a downturn of my career, which until this point had been starry and surreal. I suppose you could say that, for the first time in my life, I was unlucky. And I was unready to face the music. I was hiding from destiny. Hiding from myself. Ultimately I came out of hiding and began to think outside myself. It's how Love works. What blesses one blesses all.

I began to shyly apply the lessons I learned about my gift of healing, the lessons of Love that lead to more of an attitude of service. For example, I had become very close with several members of a family who were all born in another country. They have tremendous talent in a wide variety of artistic endeavors and also a great deal of inherited pride. They are not the type of family that go around blurting their feelings and concerns. So it was with great worry that I met with one of the sisters who expressed to me her fear that her brother, who was a photographer and also my friend, was teetering on the verge of death because of his latest battle with a new and brutal addiction to crack.

Though I have played a few characters who used drugs–such as Jim Morrison, Danny Parker, and porn star John Holmes in the film *Wonderland*–I feel extremely grateful to say these substances have not played a role in my own story. As one of my spiritual practitioners once said of addiction, "It's not necessarily a bad motive: to get out of the pain of mortality. We're all trying to do that in various ways. The sad trapped abuser of narcotics or alcohol has just picked a technique that cannot get them to that peace." Ah, to know that peace! What an occasion and cause to celebrate, achieving that peace! Well, the request from my friend was simple. Her brother was not answering his phone or the intercom of his apartment building but the family knew he was in there. And he had been in there so long they feared this time it may be for good. He might already be dead.

This was quite a puzzle. How do you reach someone who can't be reached? How do you get them to come out of their bat cave? The first step is getting them to see how close to the edge they are dancing.

They know they are dancing with death, but do they know it might be last call and the blinding house lights are about to go on? And not the actual burning daylight of the sun, and the harsh slog back to reality it represents.

Healing is always about an early step of conquering fear. First your own, of course, then the patient's. But if the subject isn't a patient, if they haven't given their consent, you can't go knocking around in their consciousness without permission. It is akin to trespassing in someone's home. You wouldn't go into your friend's house and re-arrange the furniture in their living room. Especially if that friend is blind. That would be worse than an act of misguided Love. That would be an act of aggression.

I couldn't break down his door or bribe his landlord. I couldn't even get inside his building. So how was I going to get to him? Suddenly it hit me. I called him and, employing my best groovy hipster cool Jim Morrison hypnotic voice, started to leave a message on his answering machine: "Hey man, it's Val. Yeah, sorry to bug you but I just don't know who else to call. 'Cause I'm going to this party with this girl and really need some high-quality—"

He instantly picked up the phone.

"Heeeeeey, Vaaal. How you been? How much are you looking for, man?"

"Oh well, I don't know. I don't know measurements. Enough to make, say, four people really happy for a few days."

"Where are you? Do you have cash?"

I gave him the name and address of a nearby dive bar.

"I'll be there," he said. And then he coughed. He coughed like his lungs were going to come through the phone and get all over me.

And so I found myself at a smelly dive bar in the middle of the night trying to spread the love of Love, trying to save a life. I waited for a while. I admit several times I gave up on him showing and imagined his funeral. Then there came a slap on my back, the hand sliding over my very expensive black leather jacket and, in an exaggerated movement, gently indicating I was to bring my right hand up to grasp his right hand in a sort of handshake-massage-embrace hug, which magically culminated in his handing off to me a rather sizeable amount of cocaine. Which I pocketed like that Disneyland magician whose sleight-of-hand magic maneuvers mesmerized me as a child.

Before me stood a praying mantis in dark sunglasses, a crumpled leather coat, and three-thousand-dollar black denim from Japan. Two women were with him. They were thin as rice paper, too, and functioning I would guess on day number three or four of a mad drug run. I couldn't quite figure out whether the shorter of the two tall women was wearing any sort of top. She seemed to have covered herself in various kinds of feather boas that made up a sort of top but really they were more like a garnish. They introduced themselves but their indeterminate accents made their names intelligible. It was as if they were speaking a secret vampire language.

I whispered to my friend, "I'll meet you outside in two minutes." Then I went to the bathroom and flushed the drugs down the toilet, hoping it wasn't going to break my bank to pay for it.

Outside the bar, I led him away from the girls and into a side alley. I dropped the hipster-stoner voice and said, "I came to find you."

I saw by the look in his eyes that it was game over. He knew everything and was not about to stand there for even thirty seconds and be lectured by his sisters through me. I boxed him into a doorway so he couldn't escape. He smelled like death. *Get to it, Val, and let Love rule. Let Love rule your entire being and your heart and mind and tongue.*

"It's not just your sisters. There are a lot of people out here who don't want to see you die. I'm one of 'em. I am about to start a new film. Maybe I can get you a job as the set photographer. It's a medium-size film so the pay might be pretty good. What is the name of the girl that doesn't seem to be wearing a top? She looks familiar."

"She designs clothes."

"Well, she forgot to put them on."

"No, she didn't. Why, you like her? Take her."

"No, no, nothing like that. We all want you to not die. And I know this is really hard to hear, but you need to let us help you not die. You have to let the people who love you, love you. It's worth it. Believe me."

Well, he did. He made a full recovery. He did a few specialty shoots for films I was in, and ended up getting married and has two beautiful children and never sees vampires anymore.

So yes, I've seen redemption in my life. The only thing holier than a crucifixion is a resurrection.

Kiss Kiss Kiss Goes the Indie,
Bang Bang Bang Goes the Downey

(Sung to the tune of Judy Garland's "The Trolley Song")

R eality kept demanding I get gigs that paid. I haven't counted how many movies I've made. I don't want to, because for a long period of time, I had to make movies for money. There are worse things I could've done.

Yet I have here described myself as a man with lofty goals, and I have a solid two decades' worth of work that I'd describe as less than lofty. On the other hand, I was blessed that in this extended period more than a few scintillating scripts came my way. When they did, I grabbed them. One of them came a little before the films I've just mentioned.

Robert Downey Jr. and I had met only once on a long evening, when during an awards dinner we circled one another like Holliday and Ringo. Everyone knew of Robert's struggles with addiction and pain. The studios had steered clear of him because he was uninsurable. He had hit bottom. But he had also gotten clean. All I knew was that Robert's brain was a masterpiece of creativity. He was smart as a whip.

Shane Black was willing to take a chance on Robert and convinced his producers to cast him in the lead of *Kiss Kiss Bang Bang*. A few days later, CAA called and asked me to read the script written by Shane. He had become one of Hollywood's hottest screenwriters after penning *Lethal Weapon* at just twenty-two years old. Now he was set to make his directorial debut. (He would go on to direct *Iron Man 3* and *The Predator*). CAA was excited. After reading thirty pages, so was I. I called my agent back and spoke only two words: "I'm in."

The first day of rehearsal, I introduced myself properly to Robert. We riffed and then rehearsed. But I could never stop laughing. Even when we started shooting. I've never been so unprofessional; I've never ruined so many takes in my life as I did on that film, just because I couldn't stop laughing. Robert was a lightning-fast, off-the-wall wit. We had great flow. Ever since I sat in awe of *The Kentucky Fried Movie* as a kid, I've understood comic rapport is one of the greatest joys an actor can experience. Robert facilitated that experience for me in remarkable fashion. He's an actor with the sensitivity of an artist and the mind of an academic.

His character, Harry Lockhart, was the leading man, and mine his buddy, an openly gay detective named Perry van Shrike but referred to as "Gay Perry." I wanted to unpack and unlearn every gay cliché that Hollywood had slammed in our faces over the years and play him as a man, a great detective, who happened to love other men. The film turned out to be a hoot. If it's now seen as a cult classic, the reason may be its meta nature. I've always been drawn to meta, as in *metaphysical* or *metaphor* or *metamorphosis*. *Meta* basically means "self-reflective." *Kiss Kiss Bang Bang* could be described as a meta noir, a wildly comic reflection of those delicious forties black-and-white detective melodramas complete with earnest gumshoes like Fred MacMurray and black widows like Barbara Stanwyck. Shane turned the genre on its

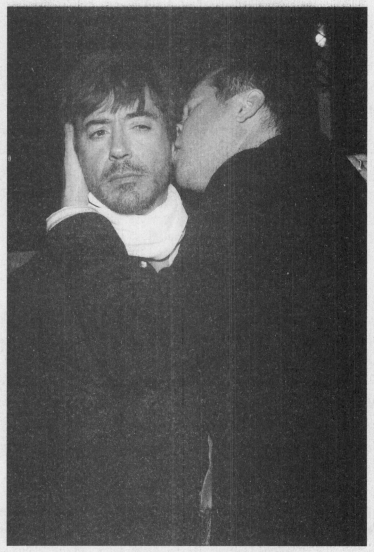

With Robert Downey Jr. at the Toronto International
Film Festival premiere of *Kiss Kiss Bang Bang*

head and morphed it into a romp that's slyly self-conscious about itself as a clever screenplay and the tradition out of which the screenplay is born.

I recently saw the film again and was reminded what Raymond Chandler, who is to noir what Louis Armstrong is to jazz, wrote in his introduction to his collection of short stories *Trouble Is My Business*. Chandler breaks down the difference between a murder mystery and a detective story. In the mystery, solving the crime is everything. But in the detective story, it's all about great scenes. "The scene," wrote Chandler, "outranks the plot." Shane understood that. So did Robert. But Robert took those scenes one step further. He played them with such bold athleticism that when *Kiss Kiss Bang Bang* proved successful, his career took off in another direction. He crushed it with *Iron Man*. A super-actor became a superhero, and I couldn't have been happier.

Other films of mine are less remembered but remain close to my heart. *Bloodworth* came and went with little notice, but I dearly cherish the moment in which my character, a bad-boy neglected son, faces his father. His father is the immortal Kris Kristofferson, a composer whom Willie Nelson justifiably ranks with Gershwin. Beyond the sublimity of his singing and songs, Kris is a strong screen presence. He possesses the lanky, laid-back cool of Gary Cooper. In *Bloodworth*, he's an aging country singer who's wandered back home to face the damage he's done by deserting his family. As his son, I am the supreme sufferer. And so I, playing the profligate son, have the rare privilege of sitting by a lake next to Kris, playing the repentant father. We fish together. The lake is calm. The sun is setting. The talk is minimal. But the feeling of fishing with my make-believe father has me thinking of another father who ran in and out of my life in ways that continue to mystify me.

When Francis Ford Coppola calls, actors come running. Because I had once refused to make that run—years earlier, when I had turned down *The Outsiders*—this time I ran like hell. It was an especially strange call because it involved starring in a faux horror movie written, produced, and directed by Francis. It was *Twixt*, a film in which he asked me to star as Hall Baltimore, a fourth-rate horror novelist down on his luck. The lead actress and my wife in the film was a woman who had captured Francis's fascination and admiration: Joanne Whalley. The fact that she would play my wife, who is unhappy in our marriage, was not a drawback. We had resolved our custody dispute to the point where the kids were spending time with both of us. I actually liked the idea of working with Joanne again. (By the way, Francis is unabashedly bonkers for Joanne, who he told me he thought of as a modern-day Clara Bow.)

When it came to marital discord, Joanne and I certainly knew the territory. The additional fact that Edgar Allan Poe, inventor of the horror genre, would be following me about in ghostly form was also attractive. I'd have some great scenes with the brilliant Bruce Dern, and because Francis was doing it on a shoestring budget entirely at his own property in Clearlake, a hundred miles north of San Francisco, it looked like an easy shoot. It wasn't.

Back in 1986, Francis's twenty-two-year-old son, Gio, was killed in a speedboat accident. My character, the down-and-out hack novelist, experienced the same pain when his daughter died in a similar accident. The scene of her death is an ongoing visual motif. My character suffers in ways that Francis suffered. My character feels the heavy weight of guilt that Francis felt. Francis admitted as much during the press conference that publicized the movie. He explained that parents, no matter the circumstances, are never free from the guilt of not being able to save their child. I think of my own dad and my brother Wesley.

I might also mention that I was friends with Gio's last girlfriend, the chic costume designer Jacqui de la Fontaine Getty. We had met while she and Gio were dating but in a rough patch. At a certain point I realized she had initially wanted to be my friend just to make Gio jealous. I was anxious to make sure Gio knew I had nothing to do with generating troubles between him and his girl. She had only told me they were a couple once we were out on a date, and the date ended at that moment. Eventually, it was all breezy between the three of us.

One summer, I was in DC filming my documentary on the nuclear dilemma and set up a meeting with Gio to tinker with and gush over a brand-new thing at the time: playback and editing on video cameras. We had a date set but he blew me off and went out on a speedboat with friends instead. That was the day he died. Francis's life was more of an opera than all three *Godfather* films combined. His son was gone. Strange miracle: three months later, Jacqui discovered she was pregnant with Gio's child. Francis and Ellie (his rock-steady wife) were over the moon. Jacqui was adopted into the family, and Gia was born.

Life's circular poetry: Gia is now a dear friend and collaborator to my son, Jack.

In any case, *Twixt* was an attempt to deal with Francis's guilt. He told me he was supposed to see Gio that fateful morning but overslept, and was haunted still by the thought that he might have saved his son had he been on the boat. The film, Francis told me, was based on a recurring dream in which Francis woke up before he could figure out the ending. For all its shortcomings, and there are many, it was nonetheless a noble and brave attempt by Francis to give dramatic life to demons that had been haunting him for so long.

Then there was *Déjà Vu*, directed by my old friend Tony Scott. I jumped at the chance to work with him again as well as with the remarkable Denzel Washington. What a treat to finally hang with Denzel in a deeper way than chatting for a few minutes while dropping our kids off at the Center for Early Education. I admire not only his dedication to his craft–he's among the finest actors of his generation–but his devotion to theater and the work of the immortal August Wilson. And perhaps most of all for the work his foundation does for the Boys & Girls Clubs of America.

I make mention of two other films, neither masterpieces, that nonetheless gave me the pleasure of working with Curtis Jackson,

With 50 Cent at the American Music Awards in Los Angeles, 2009

a.k.a. 50 Cent. Our movie *Streets of Blood* was a cop flick set in New Orleans in the aftermath of Katrina. Curtis turned out to be not only a kind and gentle man but a mighty good actor. (And his own memoir, *Get Rich or Die Tryin'*, is one of the best entertainer memoirs I've ever read.) I watched him hone his natural-born chops while he indoctrinated me into the current verbal histrionics of hip-hop, an art form I initially came to appreciate through the stupendous work of Nas, Tupac, and Biggie. Many of its practitioners today—Kanye West and Kendrick Lamar, to cite two—are artists with dazzling poetic powers. Like Curtis, they are among our most soulful storytellers.

Curtis returned the favor. Acknowledging my willingness to give him a few acting tips, he rewarded me with a 1965 Impala convertible. This was a man who clearly understood me. Curtis and I had such an easy rapport we reunited on a second film, *Blood Out*, where Curtis is a big-city detective while I play an unredeemable scumbag operating in the world of human trafficking. I strolled into the film's final scene, my hair down to my shoulders, my nefarious empire on the verge of collapse, and thought about what Marlon might have done at such a moment. He'd have smiled. Which is just what I did. Sometimes B movies are a blast.

POEMS ARE MADE BY FOOLS

Walking down to where the first tree
Met the first leaf
I search for the primitive spoor
Of me.
Setting north
We go back and forth
There are no walls to the sea.

—Okavango Delta, Botswana, 1987

Land

L ike my father, I was unstoppable. I was swallowed by Mother
Earth. The land called to me, from her armpit or her belly, and I
answered. For how could I not? Who was I, a mere mortal, to disobey
her? No. That was simply not an option. Some of us know how to walk
away. From money. From heartache. The Kilmers, though, stay, and
stay, and then stay some more.

I think of THE Juilliard. Of Japan. Of artistic merit. And then I think
of the rust belt. Of America. What is art, and who is it for? What did I
give up?

I knew which movies would be good before I took the roles. I knew
exactly how much money they would make. I've always been good
at numbers games. But I had a life outside of work. Twain says, "The
world owes you nothing. It was here first." We all have to pay our dues.
It just so happens I had to pay mine at this strange, warped midpoint
in my life, rather than right at the beginning.

I had a vision from the time that I was a kid. The dream was to
create a commune. A place where artists and believers in profound

ideas would congregate and live. The dream was based on this nonlinear sense of time and space. Come whenever, stay forever. I imagined investing in Picassos and Giacomettis and Basquiats and then letting friends and neighbors rent or borrow them. A time-share, in the truest sense. An everything-share. If you were having an engagement party and wanted to impress some city friends, you could display all the collective art on your property as you wished.

The dream appeared to be coming true. A few comrades had become family. Sam Shepard, in all his grit and glory; Gordo, in all his regal majesty; Betty and Jane, the platonic lover ladies who had brought me to the wilderness in the first place, their plain names a disguise for their strange and wild beauty.

The commune I drafted in my mind and heart would put Marfa, Texas, to shame. My land for this commune had streams and brooks that glistened in the heat. Some gorgeous estates have two or three such waterways. Well, on my land there were eleven. Can you imagine anything more blissful or holy? I cannot.

There were over a hundred domestic pets as well as beloved creatures from towering bison to rabbits, from llamas to horses to pigs and goats. And then the wildlife. A mountain lion lying in the sun by the river, just for fun. A cougar spotting me spying him and then bounding up a dry arroyo from boulder to boulder, as majestic as the USS *Enterprise*. Those cats dancing on the riverbed are as important to me as any Love I've ever known. Have you seen a hummingbird's silver glow? I have seen it, and I see it still in the eyes of my children, huddled up without making a sound, while the sleek and rarely seen fox eats the spilt bird food that has fallen in the night by the wind. I am trying in this perfect silence to teach my children something they could never know otherwise. What is the spirit of the fox, really? They are not the thieves made out to be in children books, no. Oh, if I could only come up with it for my children. Then out of the silence it is Mercedes who offers us the rare truth, whispering, "They are the perfect blend of dog and cat." Yes, that is it, you perfect child on this perfect moonlit night. You have captured the magic for us all. Shame on all of us who cannot trust ringtail raccoons on our property for a single evening. Even more shame on the manufacturers of man-made winds that kill bald eagles soaring through the sky. We must even stop the butterfly, stick it with pins and frame it. These are the things that matter to me now, and they were the things that mattered then.

I mismanaged my money and wound up broke. You've heard the excuses before—Dad's debt, divorce—but those excuses don't begin to excuse the real reason.

I called Coppola. "Francis, I feel like a fool. I'm going to have to sell my ranch. It was this utopian dream. It was unrealistic. How will I ever forgive myself?"

He calmly said, "Val, you have to stop beating yourself up. Artists take risks. That's what we do. My own flops are legendary. You'll have your art community, Val. Mark my words."

I smiled. I got out of bed. I started problem solving. The property was worth thirty million dollars, and I owed twelve.

Improbably and fortunately, I had befriended Hank Paulson, once head of Goldman Sachs and secretary of the treasury under George W. Bush. It took Hank to set me straight. He saw what was coming.

"I don't want to impinge on our friendship," I told him half a year into the recession, "but I need financial advice."

That's all I had to say.

"You're looking for a buyer for your wildlife preserve, aren't you?" asked Hank.

I said yes, and he told me the dead-serious truth: there were probably no more than twelve people in the universe wanting a gigantic parcel of land in New Mexico, and he knew every one of them. Because he was a wildlife guy, and he knew all the wealthy wildlife guys—fly-fishermen specifically. He said, "All the guys that could buy your ranch, or would, are trying to sell theirs. They won't get half. If anyone offers you half, take it. Half is the new hundred percent. How much is it appraised for?"

"It's worth thirty million dollars," I said, "and it has six miles of private river."

"How much is it against?" he asked, referring to my mortgage and loans.

"Twelve."

"Any offers?" he asked.

"One."

"How much?"

"Fifteen."

"Take it."

"But, but, but, that means I'll wind up making a measly—"

"And you'll be lucky, Val. Take the fifteen and run. Our old world is over."

I ran.

And I wound up in Malibu.

In a quaint and modest cottage by the majestic, sparkling sea, with dolphins literally flipping outside my front door.

Living in moderation in Malibu was a very practical move, to be followed by a majestically impractical one. This time, though, I scored. I put the rest of the money into my man Mark Twain and finishing my one-man show about him, *Citizen Twain*, which I intended to eventually turn into a screenplay for a film I would write, direct, produce, and star in.

I had once been circling around and dreaming about the idea of

Cate Blanchett playing Mary Baker Eddy in the film. I'd been writing about Twain and the founder of Christian Science. We were on the set of a very respected director and having lunch in the makeup trailer. I said to her I couldn't give her the script just yet. As far as proof of the quality of the production, she should see my one-man show ASAP, which she promised to do. This was before I lost my voice. I had been praying for guidance, about how one Mind directs us all, and with her husband a director also and me being so old to start directing, I thought suddenly to simply explain what my strengths were. I whispered to her, "Cate dear, I swear on my life this is what I will bring to you every hour of every day: a room that's quiet and waiting for you, waiting for you to enter that safe place, where you are able to do the best work of your life." Almost instantly she looked up and away and began to weep. I held her hand. It is one of my most treasured moments on a film set even though the camera was half a mile away. Finally, she wiped her tears away with a tissue I had gotten her and she whispered to me by way of an apology, "I can't remember the last time that's happened."

I also thought of Meryl Streep. In a very vivid dream once, in a pitch and plea for her to play my Eddy, I promised Meryl a witch's spell of endless youth and beauty. She took the Dorian Gray-style bargain, and I delivered. The mystical deal was sealed. I awoke, but the dream remained.

At this point, I had been working on both the one-man Twain play and the Twain-Eddy film script for fifteen years. If I could play a euphoric Jim Morrison or a comedic Doc Holliday, if I could be faceless Elvis or insane John Holmes, I could surely be Mark Twain. And I was. I created him with all the ferocity at my command, this man on the fringes of society and in the center of celebrity, mocked, misunderstood, lionized, belittled, emboldened by the bravery of indiscretion, reduced by mismanagement of entrepreneurial dreams. An American through and through. *The* American. Thinking these thoughts, day after day, year after year, running off to make B movies to pay the bills, I walked the beach at Malibu. Mark Twain walked with me.

I was having dinner with friends when I ran into Robin Williams, who buzzed around the restaurant to eight different tables, allowing the electric lightning bug inside to lead him on. His brilliance blinded the room. I saw Robin as Twain's son. Twain was like that. Inspiration struck and kept on striking. I completed the one-man Twain play as I worked on draft after draft of the Twain-Eddy script. Twain would have to stand alone first. He was, I saw, a stand-up comic. That was the form of the show I crafted. I found makeup wizards to transform me. I found art houses willing to let me workshop. Audiences were loving it. I'd never been happier.

Before performing a full-tilt version, I wanted a more elaborate warm-up. The opportunity came from a woman who managed the singer-songwriter Ryan Adams. She was panicked. Ryan was headlining the Walt Disney Concert Hall that night, and the opening act had canceled. Disney Concert Hall had recently opened in all its post-structuralist Gehry gravitas, and it was a big deal. The manager was calling for help. I racked my brain to think of musicians I knew who were in town. I drew a blank. And then I heard myself say what needed to be said.

"I'll open as Mark Twain."

"What? What are you talking about, Val?"

"I'll call my makeup team. They'll work their magic and turn me into Mark. I've been workshopping a one-man show with me as Twain. It'll be weird. It'll be funny. No one will forget it. Trust me."

And amazingly, she did.

I was unrecognizable as Val. I went onstage screaming highlights from the show, inventing on the spot. I riffed about Walt Disney and

As Mark Twain in *Citizen Twain*

America and the ridiculous grandeur of the space. And I got deep. "The two most important days in your life are the day you are born and the day you find out why." I had done enough theater to know I had the audience. I paused and bowed. They roared. And the announcer, satisfied, declared, "Thank you. Val Kilmer as Mark Twain." In that moment, fulfilling some sort of cross-generational destiny, I was at peace.

I toured groovy theaters and landed in a culminating few weeks at the storied and relaxed Pasadena Playhouse. The show begins with Twain coming back to the USA today, drunk as all hell but sharp as a tack. "They say living in California adds ten years to your life . . . I think I'll spend them in New York." He returns to earth because he must offer an apology to Mrs. Eddy for lying about her being a plagiarist, which he did, and also because, like myself, he's in need of applause: "I was born modest but it wore off." When the audience claps, he admits, "Aw, that's like angels lickin' me." He also has plenty to say about the state of the world, his caustic wit is a breath of fresh air. "It ain't those parts of the Bible that I don't understand that bother me. It's the parts that I do understand." He preaches; he pontificates; he evokes Mrs. Eddy: "Happiness is spiritual, born of truth and love. It is unselfish; therefore it cannot exist alone, but requires all mankind to share it." Twain is irreverent, finally getting the chance to talk back to a rude grade school teacher. When she asks all the idiots in the classroom to stand up, he stands up. His teacher looks at him and asks, "Why do you feel you are an idiot?" He replies, "Well actually ma'am, I don't. I just hate to see you standing up there all by yourself." The audience howled. As writer, director, producer, and star, I had my mojo back, all thanks to Mark.

I've always loved one-person shows. The best actor I have ever seen on Broadway was in a one-person show: Bruce Springsteen. I went to see it four times. Who else could tell the story of rock and roll like that? He's the only one who could take up that mantle. The story (the history of rock and roll) could not be told until now. He's the only one honest enough to get the job done. The Boss left his body, sweat, and soul on the stage. He testified openly. He was startlingly good. I remain inspired by his purposeful candor and storytelling wizardry.

With Bruce Springsteen after a performance of *Springsteen on Broadway*

GIVE OVER TO THE CAUSE

Rock & rollers are suckers for love
And I'm trying to get out of here to make the gig
But she's crying in the bathroom at Hollywood and Vine

She wants us to step back
Not to coalesce
To progress

Of course, none of it matters
As the sun rises and we bow in reverence and celebrate her eternal charms, our
eternal mother, our masterpiece, our reverie
I'm not confused
I'm just singin' the blues

I will wait for you.

—Hollywood, California, 2019

Glory & Gore

L ife in my Malibu cottage was the one thing my life had never been: calm. I'd stay up reading a biography of Samuel Beckett or watching CNN, fall asleep to the sound of gentle waves, wake up, and write about Twain. Cher would wander over for coffee, or I would meet her at her palace, where we'd sit on the patio and survey the gentle Pacific. The postman and local burrito man were my friends. I was a weirdo beach bum, and it was bliss.

Then bliss turned to mayhem.

It happened one fateful day when my body rebelled. This was sometime after the medical emergency I described at the start of this story when Cher put me in an ambulance.

I coughed up coagulated blood.

I presumed this was the day of my death. I was alone. But I was not alone. Strange as it sounds, I felt like a fighter who trains his whole life for a big match. I heard Twain say to me, "The fear of death follows from the fear of life. A man who lives fully is prepared to die at any time."

I really truly believed in God, and this was my chance to prove it. I was both frightened and empowered. Grounded and yet already in angelic flight, shocked but not terrified. What to do, who to choose for this call of calls—my children or my spiritual practitioner? I phoned the practitioner. We quietly prayed, and I felt an instant wave of calm wash over me. I told her it seemed practical to call an ambulance since I could not tell how much blood I had lost and it was hard to move. We prayed a bit more, then she said, "Call your children from the ambulance."

"Of course," I said. "I love you."

"I love you, too."

Because my aerie home was hidden from the highway, I knew the first responders would drive right past it. I looked up at these giant wooden stairs that led to PCH as blood dripped down my body, my vision blurred, my energy drained.

I called for the ambulance and then crawled, belly on the wood, up those steps and made it to the top, with several dozen splinters to prove it. Even then, the ambulance drove right past me. I called 911 again. Finally, the ambulance located me. I was barely able to stand. When they put me on a stretcher and got me inside, they kept yapping about their recent bowling tournament. I was hardly reassured.

I don't remember anything after. I woke up at a hospital in Santa Monica. I was given a hotshot doctor who was full of himself. I told him as much. He told me that a tracheotomy was required. That meant drilling a hole in my windpipe. We had a swift decision to make, and we made it.

Cher insisted on making a few calls. She used to be David Geffen's girl, and David has a hospital. I was transferred to UCLA and put under the care of the brilliant Dr. Maie St. John, supervisor of the head and neck division. She was wonderful and suggested chemotherapy and radiation. I went along with the program, mainly to reassure my children I was doing everything "humanly" possible to be healthy. They had been constantly taught by others in their lives to be wary of Christian Science, and although they had each had several extraordinary healings in my opinion, I respected their skepticism and did not wish to increase their fear in any way.

While I was in the hospital, I ushered Twain and Mrs. Eddy into the room. I allowed audiotapes of their books to wash over me. I let the sound waves swallow me whole. I filled the starkness of the room with a symphonic swell of knowledge and healing. I prayed. I didn't wrestle with my angels. I sang and danced with them.

Eventually I was able to put pen to paper. I wrote poems. I reread Twain, remembering what is perhaps his most famous line: "The report of my death was an exaggeration." I was indeed alive and, after two months in the hospital, had regained my energy. The fact that my impeded speech could spell the end of my career only served to motivate me. Voice was my central means of creating art. What was I going to do? I called on Wesley to get me through. Wesley arrived. He reminded me that visual art was a medium we'd explored much of our young life. I'd always painted. Painting had gotten me through the stiffness of THE Juilliard School, staying up at all hours and painting canvases on the floor or forgoing canvas and painting right on the walls, letting out my inner Jackson Pollock. I started to reach for pads in the hospital room and draw on them, and then asked my kids to bring me tools—a canvas, some magazines to rip pages from, some paints, and a material that would soon become close to my heart, perfectly neon-pink production tape.

I started ripping and shredding and searching and cutting and sewing and taping things back together. I got in trouble for getting paint and Sharpie marks all over the hospital sheets but didn't care.

I saw them as canvases. Those paintings included pieces of poems, truncated scripture, random thoughts writ large, proclaiming, "The heart feeds the head and the head seeds the harmonies."

When it was time to check out, I rented a small house in Brentwood that turned hyperactive in a hot hurry. The house became an art factory. I needed help renovating the place and hired a friend whom I called Juan the Magic Man. He started spackling and painting and tinkering and building, and, miracle of miracles, his movements mirrored mine. I asked if he'd be willing to help with my artwork, cutting wooden boards or finding scrap metal in alleys with me, or spray-painting large makeshift canvases. Juan was in. Together, we started making more art than the Brentwood cottage could house, and after a few raw social media posts, we realized there was a market for my art. I suddenly saw my designs as my means of survival.

I wasn't sure if people actually liked them or just wanted something made by Val Kilmer, but I didn't care. It was money in the bank for myself and my family, and I was doing what I loved. We hired a few other hardworking folks to set up our all-of-a-sudden art business and became the merry band of misfits I had imagined would fill my life on my forlorn land in Santa Fe. Old theater friends reappeared and never left. Things hummed along. And just when it seemed like the whole operation might close down because of our growing overhead and sagging sales, dumb luck appeared in the form of a serious art collector who fell in love with my work and bought a truckload of paintings and collages. We were back in business.

Denial vs. Denial

The insatiable paparazzi were working overtime to get the low-down on my condition. I was too busy making art to mess with the press. If they caught me leaving my place, I'd simply tell them the truth: I'd been healed. The cancer was gone. I didn't have cancer. Reports emerged that I was in denial. Well, denial is a funny thing. I was not denying that I had had cancer but was simply saying I no longer did. And to be honest, it was very hard to embrace my original diagnosis. It was surreal. I didn't believe I was decomposing, and I wasn't ready to die. I am not among those who deny the notion that God can heal today just as Jesus healed in his day. I do not deny miraculous healing.

Enter Brad Koepenick, Wesley's childhood filmmaking friend and the third beautiful wheel in my relationship with Mare Winningham. I could see Wes in his eyes. He had long left Chatsworth to become a respected producer and then sort of a luminary in theater as applied arts. In an era of fame and no Facebook, we had simply lost touch until he knocked on my door.

With Tribeca Film Festival cofounder Craig Hatkoff (*left*) and Bradley Koepenick
at the NOVUS SDG Moonshots Summit held at the United Nations, 2019

"Val, I've been looking for you. Don't say anything. I have something for you. I've found these old audiotapes and books on Mary Baker Eddy. I want you to have them. It feels like a sign. They're for you."

I was silent. I could say nothing but, "Yes."

We welcomed each other back and worked together to orchestrate an extensive Twain tour.

I twisted and Twained my way around the country, screening a filmed version of my Pasadena Playhouse performance at comedy clubs and theaters, followed by elaborate and interactive Q & As, for which I appeared fully in character. The play *Citizen Twain* became the evening of on-screen and off-screen mayhem we called *Cinema Twain*. I was basking in the bliss of a healthy obsession.

Yet Twain wasn't created to live on the margins of society, just for know-it-alls and cinephiles. No, we had to bring this to the Twains of the world. The rebels. The teenagers who hated school and craved revolution. We created the Twainmania Foundation, and with the help of some of Brad's former students and mentees, we developed a curriculum and vowed to bring it to schools in the most remote and forgotten corners of the country. Our goal was to ask youth from every gender and race to write responses to Twain, new-age manifestos on life in America. What does it mean to be a real American? We were resurrecting the Mad Missourian. We were resurrecting ourselves.

Through Twainmania, we also helped support other organizations such as the Educational Theatre Foundation, which provides theater in underserved schools across America, and Get Lit, which encourages teen literacy through spoken word and poetry. There are those who talk and those who get things done. We got things done. For this work, I was honored with the Tribeca Film Festival's Disruptive Innovation Award and an invitation to speak at the NOVUS SDG Moonshots Summit, held at the United Nations Headquarters in New York.

Our prayers had been answered. Our collective work now represented our best selves: the curriculum; a foundation; visits to schools; new opportunities for educators and students; an ongoing conversation on media literacy, Love, tolerance, and empathy through the eyes of America's true patriot, the unofficial narrator of the United States.

The Iceman Cometh Again

I was well enough to go back to making movies. I was cast as a homicidal weirdo in the horror film *The Super*. Fortunately, my speaking part was limited and my rough voice worked well with the character. The movie unapologetically bites off the setting of Polanski's *Rosemary's Baby*, a creepy but elegant New York apartment building. Though the B film contains all the trappings of its genre, I found a spiritual gift in what otherwise might be seen as a forgettable role. My character lives with unbearable anguish and unnamed suffering. He became a vehicle for my own anguish and pain. I was able to get the bad stuff out of me and put it in him. And then, oddly enough, the film's "clever" plot twist is that this superintendent, this frightening figure of moral debasement, turns out to be not a villain at all, but merely an amusing sideshow. I didn't mind participating in such sideshows.

Actors thrive on work–virtually any acting work. But when there is work that might actually revive their troubled careers, actors become beasts who will beat back the world rather than miss the chance to do such work. That was my gut reaction when I learned Tom Cruise wanted a follow-up to *Top Gun*. He was calling it *Top Gun: Maverick*. Well, Tom was Maverick, but Maverick's nemesis was Iceman. The two went together like salt and pepper. It didn't matter that the producers didn't contact me. As the Temptations sang in the heyday of Motown soul, "ain't too proud to beg." I'd not only contact the producers but create heartrending scenes with Iceman. Forget the fact that thirty years had passed since I'd seen the ghost of Iceman's dad. I remembered it like it was yesterday. The producers went for it. Cruise went for it. Cruise couldn't have been cooler. And the next thing I knew I was back, as the Beatles said, where I "once belonged." Tom and I took up where we left off. The reunion felt great. As far as the film's plot goes, I'm sworn to secrecy.

HelMel

I wanted to take the money from *Maverick* and get a gallery space. I fell in love with a quaint storefront in almost hip East Hollywood on the corner of Melrose and Heliotrope, thus the name HelMel. There was also a giant abandoned warehouse next door, large enough to house a good-size theater.

Then a vision took over, a spirit that commanded me to go for both spaces. We would have offices and a technological hub for the Twainmania Foundation. We would have a proper gallery where our art and the art of those we admired would be displayed in an elegant setting. In the theater, we would host concerts and plays and lectures and film screenings and poetry readings and dance parties. I would save money to build up my New Mexico ranch–I'd managed to keep two hundred acres–and finally make my Twain/Eddy movie.

HelMel became a reality. We penned our mission statement and painted it on the wall. *HelMel is a fun, sacred space where eclectic artists gather to collaborate and, through new technology, inspire giving and spark change in our local community.* And pell-mell, muses, friends, and collectors came calling. They seemed to find the space by chance or by destiny. Our intimate but lively gallery was soon filled with giant paintings of Bowie and charcoal drawings of the Chateau Marmont by Eric Nash, Polynesian pop art by Bosko Hrnjak, and work by so many other bright young minds, as well as myself, the old dude makin' it happen.

One night we had a group show, and the whispers were all around. *Dylan might come.* I sat in my favorite office chair, looked through our skylight in our spotless refurbished warehouse space, and exhaled so deeply I almost fainted. This was what I had always wanted. An enclave in which bohemians and pirates and academics and lovers could congregate and make things and connect. They say when one

HelMel Studios & Gallery, Los Angeles

of your five senses is compromised, you can feel the others become heightened. My speech was compromised, but I was seeing and feeling things I had never seen or felt before.

Why? I suppose that's simply the way the world works.

And we just do not know what is ahead.

Uncertainty, I realized, is holy.

Death may come.

Dylan may come.

And there isn't much we can do about it. Except sit back, breathe, and enjoy looking at the sky.

There are afternoons in my home high above the Hollywood Bowl when I watch the setting sun and reflect on friends who are gone. Sometimes I laugh from the memories. Sometimes I cry. I think of Marlon Brando. I think of David Warrilow. I think of Gordon Miller. I think of Sam Shepard. I think of Tony Scott.

I think of my mother.

She died last summer at a glorious ninety-three in her longtime home in Wickenburg, where she had become royalty. I love and miss her a lot, even though she was really tough on her two remaining boys. Locals we're still in touch with in Wickenburg always say how often she spoke so lovingly and fondly of us. I am not so puzzled about this aspect of her inability to relay this Love. It's a mysterious attribute the Swedes seem to own. They seem to like to be blue. Maybe it's the weather up there. Mom's life had been uneven, but her faith had been constant. She had bequeathed that faith to me. Some say you choose your parents. Some say you are given the parents you need. I needed my mother badly. I needed her before the cataclysmic divorce from Dad and I needed her after. I needed her always. I need her still. Today I wear her turquoise necklaces to keep her close to my heart.

With Mom at the premiere of *The Saint*, 1997

Then only a few weeks ago I lost my dear friend Robert Evans. How I loved Bob! To provide levity after his devastating stroke, I proposed the first all-male heterosexual marriage. Proposal rejected, but I did manage to get him laughing. He was one of the youngest studio heads in history–and the sharpest–who regally commanded the best office on the Paramount lot for three decades. Bob also saw himself as a great filmmaker, though he never directed and didn't know which end of the camera to look through. During those post-stroke days, I visited him at the UCLA hospital, where he was encased in tubes and could barely speak.

"What do you want?" I asked. "What can I get for you?"

A long and ominous pause. And then his answer, drawn out for what could have been days: "Cocaine."

He and I laughed so hard he almost blew the tubes out of his head.

Bob was the last grand ring-
leader in Hollywood history.
I was so fortunate that he understood me.

So have the women in
my life. I miss the company
yet am not unhappy. In some
ways, Daryl felt like the end
of that whole piece of my
personality. We loved deeply
and fought deeply and every
day with her was that unique
once-a-decade spring when
there's a beautiful storm followed by a priceless rainbow, the eternal ribbon of
hope that once established as
part of your day you cannot
live without. When we finally
broke up, I cried every single

Robert Evans takes calls by his home
pool in Beverly Hills, 1978

day for half a year at least, until I became very concerned about my
kids seeing me that way. I thought, *Grow up.* I couldn't do it anymore,
and I couldn't do it to them. I am still in love with Daryl but I joke that
she really did play the lead in *Attack of the 50 Ft. Woman,* and that's
just how I felt. Spent. It was no great surprise that she wound up marrying Neil Young. It was a matter of one giant attracting another.

Those kind of rip-your-heart-out relationships that had become so
normal for me were just no good anymore. Love was at the core of my
life, that was for sure, but was it the kind of Love that was building
toward a life of service? My old friend Gordo, that serious student of

poetry, had a famous teacher who once reminded his most promising pupils, "With poetry you have the opportunity to refine your entire life into a single stone, and you must take every hour to press and mold the clay of your life into that stone, and then in the last half of your life just make sure you are polishing the right stone."

After Daryl, I had nothing left to give except to my church, to my kids, to my art, to my foundation, and to myself. When I stopped focusing on finding that perfect wife, that energy stream was channeled into other equally wild and mystical avenues. I longed for a deeper layer of self-exploration. I made a decision that, rather than looking for Love, I would let Love be me. Let Love be my life. Let Love seep through the pages of this, my life story.

Let it also be known that this story is far from over. I hear Robert Frost saying, "But I have promises to keep / And . . . miles to go before I sleep." I hear Twain saying, "I do not fear death. I had been dead for billions and billions of years before I was born, and had not suffered the slightest inconvenience from it." I hear Wallace Stevens saying, "At evening, casual flocks of pigeons make / Ambiguous undulations as they sink, / Downward to darkness, on extended wings."

I'm not going to pretend to know how that quote fits in here. I just like it. I wish to be those wings. I believe I am. I believe I am on a flight that, day by day, is generated by the poetry of my heart. The poetry was there from the start. It was born inside my grandmother, grandfather, father, and mother. Born inside my brother Wesley. I have his poetry and his wings. He has mine. You have mine and I have yours. Those wings, that ability to transcend the suffering of human drama, is the gift of the inaudible and invisible spirit whom we hear and see as clearly as Stevens's undulating pigeons. We see spirit in the mist and fog; we hear spirit in the silence of the stones. Polish those stones; they make a noble life possible. We feel spirit every time we love, every time we forgive, every time scorn is overwhelmed by empathy and bitterness overcome by compassion.

The song says we shall overcome. My voice will come back. If I recall, the scripture says joy will come in the morning. It isn't just that everything is going to be all right. Everything *is* all right. Right now. Right now, the energy grows. I feel it more now than at any other moment in my life. The energy allows me to channel the gratitude that drives me home and drives me to you. The energy is transferable. The energy is contagious. The energy is eloquence. I offer it to you. It is this energy, this crush on the beauty of the universe, that makes everything deeper, every act of tenderness, every optimistic thought. It is exquisite, and it isn't going anywhere. It is the energy of eternal Love.

MIND'S MOVIE

In my mind's movie
After the very last party
After the razor blades have gone home
Irena will not return
And all that's left are aesthetics
And the work is here at hand like a sundance
Like a boy dancing as the sun goes down
Right before the credits

—New York City, 1978

PHOTO CREDITS

Ron Galella, Ltd./Ron Galella Collection via Getty Images: ii, 243

Author: 10, 14, 26, 33, 93, 179, 215, 283, 298

Bettmann via Getty Images: 18

Daily Mirror/Mirrorpix/Mirrorpix via Getty Images: 21

Robert Carelli: 44, 45

Jessica Katz: 57, 65

The Asahi Shimbun via Getty Images: 69

Photo by Martha Swope © Billy Rose Theatre Division, New York Public
Library for the Performing Arts: 73

Photo © Johan Elbers 1985/Courtesy BAM Hamm Archives: 75

Dave Hogan/Hulton Archive/Getty Images: 77

TCD/Prod.DB/Alamy Stock Photo: 80, 117, 199

David Montgomery/Premium Archive/Getty Images: 82

Walt Disney Television via Getty Images Photo Archives/Walt Disney
Television via Getty Images: 85

Michael Ochs Archives/Moviepix/Getty Images: 99

Ronald Grant Archive/Alamy Stock Photos: 119, 184

LUCASFILM/Album/Alamy Stock Photo: 137

Courtesy of Colorado Shakespeare Festival: 142

Moviestore Collection Ltd/Alamy Stock Photo: 146, 150

PHOTO CREDITS

ACKNOWLEDGMENTS

Thanks to all those who helped in this literary effort: Sean Manning, David Vigliano, Veronika Shulman, Brad Koepenick, Daniel Voll, David Ritz, Mary Moran, Lisa Katz, Suzan Alparslan, Nate Talbot, Grant Hayunga, Tom Stratton, Ali Alborzi, Cher, Miguel Silva, Virginia Harris, Leo Scott, Ting Poo, and Barry Hirsch. Ongoing gratitude and boundless love to my children, Mercedes and Jack, and to countless others who have supported me with full hearts during good times and bad. And above all, I thank God.